The Public Purpose of Education and Schooling

John I. Goodlad
Timothy J. McMannon
Editors

The Public Purpose of Education and Schooling

Jossey-Bass Publishers • San Francisco

Substantial discounts on bulk quantities of Jossey-Bass books are available to corporations, professional associations, and other organizations. For details and discount information, contact the special sales department at Jossey-Bass Inc., Publishers (415) 433–1740; Fax (800) 605–2665.

Jossey-Bass Web address: http://www.josseybass.com

For sales outside the United States, please contact your local Simon & Schuster International Office.

Manufactured in the United States of America using Lyons Falls D'Anthology paper, which is a special blend of non-tree fibers and totally chlorine-free wood pulp.

Library of Congress Cataloging-in-Publication Data

The public purpose of education and schooling/John I. Goodlad, Timothy J. McMannon, editors.—1st ed.
p. cm.—(The Jossey-Bass education series)
Includes bibliographical references and index.
ISBN 0-7879-0934-3 (cloth: acid-free paper)
1. Education—Aims and objectives—United States. 2. Education—Social aspects—United States. 3. Educational change—United States. I. Goodlad, John I. II. McMannon, Timothy J. III. Series.
LA210.P83 1997
370\.973—dc21 96-45875
CIP

FIRST EDITION
HB Printing 10 9 8 7 6 5 4 3 2

The Jossey-Bass Education Series

Contents

Part Two: Conversations

Part Three: A Public Agenda?

Preface

The National Network for Educational Renewal (NNER) was established in 1986 to put into practice the belief that the improvement of schooling and the renewal of teacher education must proceed simultaneously. In short, good schools need good teachers, and good teachers need exemplary preparation—including exemplary school settings in which to learn the art of teaching. If educators try to advance either the schools or teacher preparation programs alone, the result is almost certain to be failure: poor teacher preparation undermines school improvement efforts, and poor schools negate teacher education advances. Typically, however, educational reform efforts address *either* schools *or* teacher education, but not both. The sixteen member settings of the NNER—presently embracing thirty-four colleges and universities working in collaboration with more than four hundred partner schools in over one hundred school districts in fourteen states—are committed to the simultaneous renewal strategy.

As part of their renewal effort, individuals associated with the network devote a great deal of thinking to the broad social and political implications of public schooling. They recognize the power of words and the need for precise definitions. They also concern themselves with education as a moral endeavor, not merely a technical one. Individuals who participate in the work of the network believe that good teachers must reflect carefully on their pedagogy as well as on the place of schooling in society and apply their thinking to school and classroom practices.

In this spirit of reflective professionalism, representatives and friends of the NNER gathered in New York City in November 1995 for a national conference. The centerpiece of that conference was a panel discussion moderated by John Goodlad under the title, "The Public Purpose of Education and Schooling." This book is the result of that conference. Prior to the symposium, the panelists wrote papers examining some aspect of the theme. These papers, reprinted here in slightly revised form as Chapters One through Six, were circulated among the contributors and served as the foundation from which the panel discussion grew. The discussion and the panelists' conversation with the audience that followed are transcribed with minor revisions for clarity and presented here as Chapters Seven and Eight. Essays by the editors, Timothy McMannon and John Goodlad, introduce and reflect on the whole. Finally, there is a brief appendix with annotations of selected works by the contributors and suggestions for further reading.

The Editors

John I. Goodlad is codirector of the Center for Educational Renewal at the University of Washington and president of the independent Institute for Educational Inquiry in Seattle. He is the author of *A Place Called School: Prospects for the Future* (1984), *Teachers for Our Nation's Schools* (1990), *Educational Renewal: Better Teachers, Better Schools* (1994), and *In Praise of Education* (1997).

Timothy J. McMannon teaches history at colleges and universities in the Seattle area and is a researcher with the Institute for Educational Inquiry. He wrote *Morality, Efficiency, and Reform: An Interpretation of the History of American Education*, Work in Progress Series, no. 5, Institute for Educational Inquiry (1995).

The Contributors

Benjamin R. Barber is the Whitman Professor of Political Science and director of the Walt Whitman Center at Rutgers University. His publications include *Strong Democracy: Participatory Politics for a New Age* (1984), *An Aristocracy of Everyone: The Politics of Education and the Future of America* (1992), and *Jihad vs. McWorld* (1995).

Linda Darling-Hammond is William F. Russell Professor in the Foundations of Education at Teachers College, Columbia University, and codirector of the National Center for Restructuring Education, Schools, and Teaching (NCREST). Her recent publications include *Professional Development Schools: Schools for Developing a Profession* (1994), *A License to Teach: Building a Profession for Twenty-First Century Schools* (1995), and *Authentic Assessment in Action: Studies of Schools and Students at Work* (1995).

Gary D Fenstermacher is professor of education at the University of Michigan. He edited with John Goodlad *Individual Differences and the Common Curriculum: National Society for the Study of Education 82nd Yearbook* (1983), and his writings include *Approaches to Teaching* (1986, 1992), and *Where Are We Going? Who Will Lead Us There?* (1993).

Donna H. Kerr is professor of education at the University of Washington. Her writings include *Educational Policy: Analysis, Structure, and Justification* (1976), *Barriers to Integrity* (1984), and numerous recent articles on "packaging the soul," nurture, and the role of self-understanding in education.

Theodore R. Sizer is University Professor Emeritus at Brown University, chairman of the Coalition of Essential Schools, and founding director of the Annenberg Institute for School Reform. He is the author of *Horace's Compromise: The Dilemma of the American High School* (1984), *Horace's School: Redesigning the American High School* (1992), and *Horace's Hope: What Works for the American High School* (1996).

Roger Soder is codirector of the Center for Educational Renewal at the University of Washington and vice president of the Institute for Educational Inquiry in Seattle. He coedited (with John I. Goodlad and Kenneth A. Sirotnik) *The Moral Dimensions of Teaching* (1990) and *Places Where Teachers Are Taught* (1990). He edited *Democracy, Education, and the Schools* (1996).

The Public Purpose of Education and Schooling

Introduction

The Changing Purposes of Education and Schooling

Timothy J. McMannon

What is education? What purposes does it serve? How does it benefit the person being educated? How does it benefit society? What are the differences between education and schooling? How do we know if our educational system is working? Do different levels of schooling (elementary, secondary, and postsecondary) have different purposes, or are they merely different parts of a continuum? What should teachers know? And what should they be able to do?

These are simple questions; the answers, however, are not so simple. Usually there are many answers or combinations of answers from which to choose. And as time passes, both the questions and the answers evolve in response to changes in the larger society. To complicate matters even further, there is frequently some difference between what our educational institutions are *expected to do*, what they *actually do*, and what ideally they *should do*.[1] But the difficulties inherent in such questions as these do not give us license to shy away from them. We must seek to answer them—then constantly reexamine our answers—in order to renew not only our educational system but also our teacher education programs and even our nation. But as we study the present and look to the future we must not lose sight of the past. Others who came before us also struggled with these questions, and their ideas, although intended for different eras, can provide us with guidance or warnings. To determine where we are going, it is vital to remember where we have been.

In many cultures throughout history, education was done entirely or almost entirely by institutions other than formal schools. The community, the family, and the church are but three examples of such institutions. One generation taught the next the ways of the people, including the mysteries of hunting, farming, participating in religious rites, and seeking a mate, as well as whatever reading, writing, or mathematical calculating was necessary. Such cultures considered education to be a lifelong experience. Elders were revered not simply for their ability to survive but for the wisdom they presumably had gained over the years. Even when the average life span was significantly shorter than it is now, to suggest that a person had become thoroughly educated by eighteen or twenty-two years of age would have been considered ludicrous. In short, education little resembled the formal schooling to which we in late–twentieth-century America have grown accustomed.

Although colleges and private academies have existed in what is now the United States since the early 1600s, American education largely mirrored the informal, traditional pattern until the nineteenth century. Few children received more than the barest smattering of what was called book learning. Elite colonial families sometimes hired private tutors to instruct their children, but most young people gained the necessary information and skills from family members or the larger community.

By the nineteenth century, however, a variety of forces interacted to bring formal schooling to the forefront.[2] Job specialization, industrialization, technological advance, urbanization, and similar developments increased workers' efficiency to the point that more people—among them, teachers—were able to pursue occupations not directly linked to physical survival. Work was moved away from the home, and the nuclear family replaced the extended one.[3] Knowledge, like work, became more specialized, and traditional institutions less able to educate the young thoroughly. At the same time, as populations concentrated in towns and cities, it became increasingly more efficient to bring groups of pupils together under the tutelage of a single teacher or lecturer than to rely on the family, the community, or an independent contractor to instruct each young person. The incipient democratization of schooling, particularly at the secondary level, allowed employers to raise their expectations regarding workers' preemployment preparation. By the late 1800s, a high school education became the minimum qualification for a white-collar job and the desired middle-class life that accompanied it. To fulfill the ever more challenging task of educating the young to take their places in society, therefore, formal schooling under the guidance of professional teachers became America's chosen tool, and so it remains.[4]

But what is this thing called schooling? First, it is not merely a synonym for education. A person can be educated without having been schooled, just as someone else may spend years in school, receive the requisite degrees, yet remain uneducated. In seeking to define schooling, one may be tempted to start with a list of its characteristics: students, teachers, a building or other physical space in which students and teachers meet, and tools such as books, papers, pencils, and laboratory equipment. But this enumeration does not say much about schooling itself. It is far more than the sum of its parts. Schooling is above all a process, the desired results of which are educated persons. Thus, although schooling itself is not education, the best schooling more fully *provides* education.

Like education, schooling can be a lifelong process. Teachers are required to return to the classroom periodically to update their knowledge of educational theory, subject matter, technology, and their own social roles in the school and community. Other professions and many trades place similar demands on their members, compelling them to take courses in order to keep their licenses current. Colleges and universities offer informal as well as formal continuing education classes. And many retirees go back to school out of a simple desire to learn. Typically, however, formal schooling is considered to be at an end when a student receives a high school or college diploma.[5]

Because lower levels of schooling are prerequisites for higher, it makes little sense to think of schooling as anything but a continuous process. A student advances from grade to grade in elementary school, from elementary school to high school, or from high school to college on the basis of some measure of success at each step. Later schooling builds naturally upon earlier and upon the learning that may be assumed to have taken place. Consider, for example, basic literacy. Among the first major academic tasks facing a young child is learning to read and write. A few children arrive at kindergarten or first grade with these skills, but the majority learn them in school. For the rest of a child's years in school, most learning will be based on the assumption that he or she can read and write at least to a minimum level of proficiency. Because education is a seamless process that builds on earlier learning and experience, schooling, as the means to achieve education, logically parallels it. As Ernest Boyer succinctly put it, "All educational levels are related."[6]

For a variety of reasons—some selfish, some altruistic—American governmental units have encouraged education, most often equating it with formal schooling. "Encouraged" is perhaps too weak a word; schooling has been made compulsory for American youth. As a result, in the United States today public elementary and secondary schools are available for virtually all children. (Not all children attend public schools, of course; many are in private schools or are taught at home. Nevertheless, public schools are an option for American students.) Just what goes on in each school in the myriad local districts is a product of several forces: national and state law, district policy, administrative norms of the specific school, the interest and ability of teachers and pupils, the community's financial status, and more. What all schools have in common, however, is an underlying belief that educating the young is a task that simply *must* be done. It is more than just a responsibility of one generation to the next; it is a positive good, not only for the pupils themselves but for society—indeed, for the whole human race.

What, then, is education? What *should* it be? Radio commentator Earl Nightingale once did a broadcast in which he pointed out that education enables us to enjoy the things in life that do not cost much: listening to a piece of music, viewing a work of art, reading a good book, engaging in conversation. Although a person might spend great sums of money on any one of these—by purchasing a Monet, for example, or by speaking to friends via long-distance telephone—each can be done virtually for free via radio, public concerts, public libraries, and the like. Nightingale's description of education included many more ideas than just the way it provides for low-cost entertainment, but there is a great deal of truth to even this truncated depiction of education. Truly to appreciate any one of these requires one to apply his or her own knowledge and experiences. To the uneducated mind, music may be mere noise, artworks simply agglomerations of media, books merely so much paper and ink, and conversation just the sounds of voices. Education, however, allows a person to perceive meaning in musical tones, in visual stimuli, and in the spoken and written word. In short, education enables one to participate more fully in the human conversation of which all of these are elements. When people are judged ignorant or unappreciative of cultural achievements, educational institutions are likely to be blamed. Reformers from Robert Maynard Hutchins to Allan Bloom have held schools accountable for our society's ignorance of the classics and our concomitant inability to call upon a common body of metaphors and symbols in spoken and written conversation.[7] Education, therefore, is—or should be—at least partly a process of enculturation into the human family.

But education is also a process of socialization, preparing each individual to take an active place in the specific society in which he or she lives. Society may best be understood, perhaps, as a subset of the entire human race. Members of a society have certain commonalities that set them off from nonmembers: language (or a specialized terminology), territory, traditions, experiences, institutions, activities, and so on. Many societies have rather fluid borders, and a person may move easily from one to another or be a member of several different societies at the same time. Others have such solid borders that they can be breached only with the greatest difficulty. Some societies one is born into; others admit members only after they have earned entry through achievement or experience. The society with which public education in the United States must concern itself most specifically is that composed of the country's citizens. Certainly students from other countries have attended and will continue to attend educational institutions in the United States, especially at the postsecondary level. But the socialization process that takes place in American schools must of necessity be one that prepares young people to assume their future roles as American citizens. Observed Yale President A. Bartlett Giamatti: "The purpose of education . . . is to lead us to some sense of citizenship, to some shared assumptions about individual freedoms and institutional needs, to some sense of the full claims of self as they are to be shared with others."[8] In other words, one function of education in this country is to perpetuate and reshape society.

An education that enculturates and socializes without imparting knowledge would not merit being called an education. Imparting knowledge is, of course, the main educational duty that American schools historically have been expected to fulfill. It has been and is one of the most difficult and important tasks assigned to any social institution. Today, however, schools are asked to do much more than educate. Indeed, John Goodlad has identified twelve goals that American schools are generally expected or required to assist students to reach, from "mastery of basic skills or fundamental processes" and "career education" to "interpersonal relations," "autonomy," "citizenship," "creativity," and "self-realization."[9] As Goodlad summarized: "Recent studies of schools and school districts suggest that parents have difficulty choosing among academic, social, vocational, and personal educational goals for their children. They want them all, at least for some stage of schooling."[10] The reason for this expanded role for schools is that over time other institutions—family, church, marketplace, peers—have largely abdicated their educative functions, leaving the schools solely responsible for imparting to the young not just knowledge and literacy but also morality, facility in interpersonal relationships, good hygiene habits, shopping skills, and any number of other abilities. Schools were never intended to be the sole educating institutions in American society, and in light of these other duties, their failure to teach subject matter well—if indeed they do so fail—is at least understandable, if not forgivable. When critics invariably conclude that the schools are not serving their intended purpose because mathematics test scores drop or surveys indicate that high school seniors cannot find their home states on a map, it would be well to remember that schools are no longer permitted the luxury of simply teaching academic subjects.

Neither educators nor social commentators nor students nor parents of schoolchildren have always thought of the American school as the locus of such a broad range of educational activity. Historically, the typical perception of schooling was closer to the description of a college education outlined in the famous Yale Report of 1828. That document argued that the purpose of the college was to discipline and furnish the mind, and thus to "lay the foundation of a superior education" while providing "a substitute . . . for parental superintendence."[11] To teach children how to think, to fill their minds with things to think about, and to keep them out of trouble while they are away from their parents: this trio of functions would go a long way toward pleasing any parent of a K–12 pupil today.

A long way, but not far enough: today, of the dozen goals mentioned earlier, career education is especially prominent. Students themselves, as well as their parents and the nation's business and political leaders, insist that schools provide training for the world of work. Vocationalism is particularly strong at the postsecondary level. Ernest Boyer, citing data collected in autumn 1984, reported: "Most students agree that pursuing a special field of study, one that leads to a career, is the main reason for going to college—and for staying, too. Over a third of the undergraduates at public institutions and slightly fewer of those at private ones say that if college did not increase their prospects for employment they would drop out."[12]

This sentiment is by no means new to higher education. The University of Salerno in Italy was established in the Middle Ages specifically to teach medicine, and Cambridge was created to train clerks to serve the king.[13] Harvard College, the first institution of higher education in British North America, was founded in 1636 expressly to prepare young men for the professions, especially the ministry.[14] But vocationalism long ago seeped into high schools as well. In 1911, the Committee of Nine on the Articulation of High School and College issued a report on behalf of the National Education Association in which it argued that the purpose of the high school "was to lay the foundations of good citizenship and to help in the wise choice of a vocation."[15] A 1980 survey of parents of high school children revealed that vocational training still had not lost its luster. Nearly 80 percent considered vocational preparation a "very important" goal for the high school.[16] Recent presidential leadership concerning education has also emphasized the vocational with the Clinton administration's program called "School-to-Work."

Vocationalism in American education is reinforced by a supporting logic of practicality—a logic which itself has a fairly lengthy pedigree. The most obvious characteristic of this logic is the equating of practicality with some sort of beneficial return, preferably—but not always—monetary. Henry Steele Commager's description of the typical nineteenth-century American demonstrates that the twentieth century came by its practical bent naturally. Education was the religion of the American of that earlier time, reported Commager, and—like religion—education was expected to "be practical and pay dividends."[17] To the American way of thinking, practicality or financial return has always implied goodness; impracticality has connoted waste, frivolity, or, in a word, badness.

Supporters of the idea of schools as job-training institutes use the logic of practicality to bolster their views. To be good, education must be practical; to be practical, education must prepare one for that most practical (that is, directly remunerative) of all functions: work. Any part of the educational process that does not directly prepare one for work is not practical and is therefore unnecessary—or at least expendable in times of budget shortfall. Few vocationalists, perhaps, would take such an unyielding position; most admit that some history, literature, and music is nice, too. But their main emphasis is on vocational preparation to enable the individual student to move on to the world of work when the school years are over.[18]

Vocationalism has also forced the schools repeatedly to bear the burden of patriotism and national defense. The most obvious instance followed the Soviet Union's launch of Sputnik in 1957. American schools were harangued (and paid) to emphasize mathematics and science so that the United States could overtake the U.S.S.R. in the space race. Pleased to be the target of financial largesse, if not of finger pointing for the U.S. failure to be first into space, schools rapidly adapted to the new emphasis. But as Richard Hofstadter noted, "The ruling passion of the public seemed to be for producing more Sputniks, not for developing more intellect, and some of the new rhetoric about education almost suggested that gifted children were to be regarded as resources in the cold war."[19] By the 1990s, the rhetoric had changed. The job for which schoolchildren had to be prepared was no longer saving the nation from Communist aggression but saving the nation from Japanese economic competition. The United States had to win the battle of the market, and schools were to be the boot camps.

At no time have the advocates of job preparation in schools and universities had the floor entirely to themselves. Employment alone seems to most people an insufficient aim for education, and as an alternative to this narrow vocationalism educationists have usually offered liberal education or some variation on that theme.[20] In the time of Aristotle, liberal education was understood to be that which literally liberated a person, freeing him from the constraints of manual labor and enabling him to speculate at length on philosophy and government.[21] This definition implied a large degree of exclusivity: because only a select few were actually needed to lead the populace, liberal education was only for those few. Also inherent in this understanding of liberal education was the distinction between mind and body. Just as the mind was considered superior to the body, so was liberal education believed to be superior to manual training, and working with the mind superior to working with the hands. By the time of the Middle Ages, liberal education had been formalized into the seven liberal arts: the trivium, composed of grammar, rhetoric, and logic; and the quadrivium of arithmetic, music, geometry, and astronomy. As the liberal arts became increasingly venerated with age, they came to be viewed more and more as antithetical and superior to any training or education that prepared one to do some specific work.

The United States, as heir to the European educational tradition, was also heir to this dichotomous conception of education. Oceans of ink have been spilled by the champions of liberal education on the one side and advocates of job preparation on the other. One supporter of the utilitarian, vocational role of higher education was Thomas Jefferson. He simply assumed that collegiate education was mainly preparation for work, and he saw the conflict as being between specific training for the professions and generalized training applicable to all occupations. Jefferson, ever the democrat, preferred the broader view and, as Merle Borrowman observed, "strove to make the collegiate program more directly functional in the lives of those aspiring to vocational goals other than the professions."[22] Benjamin Franklin was of much the same mind, but he saw the lower academies as the logical providers of utilitarian training.[23] Horace Mann, in the Massachusetts State Board of Education's Twelfth Annual Report (1848), put it this way: "Education then, beyond all other devices of human origin, is a great equalizer of the conditions of men. . . . It does better than to disarm the poor of their hostility toward the rich: it prevents [their] being poor."[24] In the late nineteenth century, university presidents Charles W. Eliot (Harvard), Andrew D. White (Cornell), and David Starr Jordan (Stanford) carried the banner for utility in higher education.[25] And more recently, the 1983 report, *A Nation At Risk,* began its appeal for reform with a statement that indicated just what threatened the nation. After noting in its opening sentence that, indeed, "Our Nation is at risk," the report proceeded: "Our once unchallenged preeminence in commerce, industry, science, and technological innovation is being overtaken by competitors throughout the world."[26] The clear implication of these latter-day utilitarians was not that Americans were at risk of living in ignorance, or that "Johnny can't read," but that Americans were no longer being trained to be the finest workers in the world.

Vocational training is not the only utilitarian outcome that schools have been expected to provide. Ironically, schools have also been used to bar children from the labor market and thus to protect jobs for adults. Some of the most steadfast allies of compulsory education laws, in fact, were the labor unions.[27] Another very practical goal for the schools has been to protect society: the earliest common schools in America were intended to produce good Christians and thus good citizens.[28] Schools also provide reliable babysitting services and, for many children today, the most nutritious meals they eat. Usually, however, when the practical aspects of schooling are discussed, outcomes such as these are deemphasized and job preparation is stressed.

Advocates of the liberal education point of view often respond with arguments focusing on the need to educate the whole person, to cultivate the intellect, or to encourage self-fulfillment: in short, to teach the student how to think. In one of the first great statements in America of the liberal point of view, that is, the Yale Report mentioned earlier, the president and fellows of Yale College concluded that disciplining the mind was more important than furnishing it.[29] In other words, of the two main goals of the college, teaching a student how to use his mind was paramount. A century later, Abraham Flexner wrote in *Universities: American, English, German* that "neither secondary, technical, vocational, nor popular education belongs in a university."[30] And in what might well be called the manifesto of liberal education, *The Higher Learning in America*, Robert Maynard Hutchins argued that vocationalism leads to triviality, isolation, disorder, and, ultimately, immorality. The purposes of education, he averred, were to cultivate the intellect, to draw out elements of common human nature, and thereby to teach the young not only how to reason but also how to comprehend and assimilate experience.[31]

There is often a very fine line between the vocational and the liberal. Even such proliberal theorists as the Yale faculty could not evade the utilitarian underpinnings of liberal education. The "object" of liberal education, they wrote, was

> not to teach that which is peculiar to any one of the professions; but to lay the foundation which is common to them all. . . . The great object of a collegiate education, *preparatory to the study of a profession,* is to give that expansion and balance of the mental powers, those liberal and comprehensive views, and those fine proportions of character, which are not to be found in him whose ideas are always confined to one particular channel. . . . He who is not only eminent in professional life, but has also a mind richly stored with general knowledge, has an elevation and dignity of character, which gives him a commanding influence in society, and a widely extended sphere of usefulness [emphasis added].[32]

"Profession," "influence in society," "sphere of usefulness": all of these resonate with connotations of utility.

The most thoughtful recent analysts realize that neither vocationalism nor intellectual cultivation can fully explain schooling or education in the United States today. Schools are asked, rightly or wrongly, to do far too many things to enable them to be subsumed under any one category. Moreover, the separation of liberal education from technical or vocational training is a false one. There is, in fact, much of the other in each if it is done properly. As Alfred North Whitehead stated in his 1929 collection, *The Aims of Education and Other Essays,* "There can be no adequate technical education which is not liberal, and no liberal education which is not technical: that is, no education which does not impart both technique and intellectual vision. In simpler language, education should turn out the pupil with something he knows well and something he can do well. This intimate union of practice and theory aids both."[33]

Whitehead also took issue with those who presumed to criticize any education that smacked of utility, asking: "If education is not useful, what is it? Is it a talent, to be hidden away in a napkin? Of course education should be useful," he concluded, "whatever your aim in life."[34] For Whitehead, however, the use of education did not mean its mere application to the task of earning a living. Instead, the use of knowledge was wisdom. He struggled to explain what he meant by wisdom, calling it alternately "the way in which knowledge is held" and "active mastery" of knowledge, but considered it the quintessence of education because it "transform[s] every phase of immediate experience."[35]

There is one type of education in which the question of the balance between the liberal and the technical is of particular import—that is, professional education. For doctors, dentists, attorneys, teachers, engineers, architects, and the like, it is clearly not enough simply to have knowledge; they must have the technical skills required to turn that knowledge into action. But a collection of mere tricks of the trade without the theory that undergirds them will end in disaster sooner or later.[36] And when that disaster occurs, it harms not only the professional herself or himself, but also the public, because clients place their health, safety, and overall well-being in the professionals' hands. Certainly, the entire society has a stake in professional preparation.

But beyond these obvious examples, why, ultimately, is it important whether we consider formal education to be primarily a step toward employment, a means to achieve wisdom, or something else entirely? Because the implications of our decision are profound. Not only does our answer to that question determine the form our schools will take, but it also determines what we can logically expect of teachers, parents, and such social institutions as churches, government, and the media. Lawrence Cremin pointed out the implications of the question as well as anyone can, writing:

> I would maintain that the questions we need to raise about education are among the most important questions that can be raised in our society, particularly at this juncture in its history. What knowledge should "we the people" hold in common? What values? What

> skills? What sensibilities? When we ask such questions, we are getting at the heart of the kind of society we want to live in and the kind of society we want our children to live in. We are getting at the heart of the kind of public we would like to bring into being and the qualities we would like that public to display. We are getting at the heart of the kind of community we need for our multifarious individualities to flourish.[37]

In short, we must answer questions about education as if our lives depend on them. They do.

Notes

1. These three categories have been called, respectively, the goals, functions, and aims of the schools. For a discussion of the differences among them, see John I. Goodlad, *What Schools Are For*, 2d ed. (Bloomington, Ind.: Phi Delta Kappa Educational Foundation, 1994), pp. 5–8, 46–52.
2. The following discussion is drawn from Charles Frankel, "Higher Education's Social Role," in *Higher Education and Government: An Uneasy Alliance*, eds. W. Todd Furniss and David P. Gardner (Washington, D.C.: American Council on Education, 1979), pp. 129–36. Frankel listed five circumstances that contributed to the appearance of formal schooling: "the rise of systems of class stratification and occupational specialization"; the awareness in society of the gap between inherited ways of doing things and new knowledge; the conviction that social concord and economic efficiency require that education no longer be left to informal educational processes; the dual realization that the fundamental values of the family must be transmitted and that the family, marketplace, church, and theater cannot do it alone; and the changed perceptions accompanying the diminished role and power of the family (p. 133).
3. Recent economic and social developments, however, seem to indicate that the nuclear family—with mother, father, and their children living under one roof—is likewise being replaced. The

ready availability of divorce and changing social norms regarding sex and marriage have resulted in increasing numbers of families being led by single parents.

Ironically, divorce, along with the high price of housing, sometimes results in larger family groups living together—a new kind of extended family—as single parents with children move back home to live with *their* parents.

4. Again, there are exceptions to this generalization. Home schooling, for example, has enjoyed something of a renaissance. This and similar exceptions notwithstanding, however, formal schooling still dominates the scene when it comes to teaching the young.
5. Indeed, Christopher Jencks and David Riesman argued that certifying, rather than educating, was the raison d'être of American colleges. See *The Academic Revolution* (Garden City, N.Y.: Doubleday, 1968), p. 61.
6. Ernest L. Boyer, *College: The Undergraduate Experience in America* (New York: Harper & Row, 1987), p. xi.
7. Robert Maynard Hutchins, *The Higher Learning in America* (New Haven, Conn.: Yale University Press, 1936); and Allan Bloom, *The Closing of the American Mind* (New York: Simon & Schuster, 1987).
8. A. Bartlett Giamatti, *A Free and Ordered Space: The Real World of the University* (New York: Norton, 1988), p. 213.
9. The remaining goals were "intellectual development," "enculturation," "self-concept," "emotional and physical well-being," and "moral and ethical character." Goodlad, *What Schools Are For*, pp. 46–52.
10. Goodlad, *What Schools Are For*, p. 27.
11. Portions of the Yale Report are reprinted in *Education in the United States: A Documentary History*, ed. Sol Cohen (New York: Random House, 1974), pp. 1441–51. The quotations are from p. 1443 (emphasis and capitalization omitted).
12. Boyer, *College*, p. 102.
13. For discussions of the purposes of early universities, see Charles Homer Haskins, *The Rise of Universities* (New York: Henry Holt

& Co., 1923), p. 17; and James Bowen, *A History of Western Education*, vol. 2, *Civilization of Europe: Sixth to Sixteenth Century* (New York: St. Martin's Press, 1975), pp. 109, 305.

14. See "New England's First Fruits," in Cohen, *Education in the United States*, p. 656.
15. Quoted in Richard Hofstadter, *Anti-Intellectualism in American Life* (New York: Vintage Books, 1963), p. 333.
16. Ernest L. Boyer, *High School* (New York: Harper & Row, 1983), p. 120.
17. Quoted in Hofstadter, *Anti-Intellectualism*, p. 299.
18. And some argue that this is particularly true of members of certain social strata. "In some cases," observed Christopher Jencks and David Riesman, "the 'non-academic' programs [in colleges and universities] attract the upwardly mobile because they are easy: business and education have this appeal. . . . One reason all these programs appeal to first-generation collegians is that they seem to lead directly to a job—and jobs are understandably very much on the minds of the upwardly mobile." *Academic Revolution*, p. 146.
19. Hofstadter, *Anti-Intellectualism*, p. 5.
20. The following is based on the discussions of liberal and vocational education found in John S. Brubacher, *On the Philosophy of Higher Education* (San Francisco: Jossey-Bass, 1982), pp. 75–83; and Merle L. Borrowman, *The Liberal and Technical in Teacher Education: A History of American Thought* (New York: Teachers College, 1956), pp. 3–5.
21. The male pronoun reflects the social realities of Aristotle's time: with very few exceptions, philosophers and political leaders were men.
22. Borrowman, *Liberal and Technical*, p. 41.
23. Borrowman, *Liberal and Technical*, pp. 41–42. See also John Hardin Best's introduction to *Benjamin Franklin on Education* (New York: Teachers College, 1962), p. 13.
24. Quoted in Giamatti, *Free and Ordered Space*, pp. 66–67.
25. Laurence R. Veysey, *The Emergence of the American University* (Chicago: University of Chicago Press, 1965), pp. 61, 69.

26. National Commission on Excellence in Education, *A Nation At Risk: The Imperative for Educational Reform* (Washington, D.C.: U.S. Government Printing Office, 1983), p. 5.
27. Paul E. Peterson, *The Politics of School Reform, 1870–1940* (Chicago: University of Chicago Press, 1985), pp. 15–17.
28. Borrowman, *Liberal and Technical*, pp. 34–36. See also Giamatti, *Free and Ordered Space*, p. 62.
29. Cohen, *Education in the United States*, p. 1443.
30. Abraham Flexner, *Universities: American, English, German* (New York: Oxford University Press, 1930), pp. 27–28.
31. Hutchins, *Higher Learning*, pp. 43, 100, 66–69.
32. Reprinted in Cohen, *Education in the United States*, p. 1445.
33. Alfred North Whitehead, *The Aims of Education and Other Essays* (1929; reprint, New York: Mentor, 1964), p. 56.
34. Whitehead, *Aims of Education*, p. 14.
35. Whitehead, *Aims of Education*, pp. 39–41.
36. On teaching, see John Dewey, "The Relation of Theory to Practice in Education," reprinted in *Teacher Education in America: A Documentary History*, ed. Merle L. Borrowman, no. 24 of *Classics in Education*, ed. Lawrence A. Cremin (New York: Teachers College Press, 1965), pp. 140–71.

    On architecture, see J. William Rudd, "Architecture Education: The Profundity of Edifice," in *Integrating Liberal Learning and Professional Education*, eds. R. A. Armour and B. S. Fuhrmann, New Directions for Teaching and Learning, no. 40 (San Francisco: Jossey-Bass, 1989), pp. 21–29. Note especially "Skills and Knowledge," p. 22.
37. Lawrence A. Cremin, "Public Education and the Education of the Public," *Teachers College Record* 77 (September 1975): 11.

Part One

Concepts

Chapter One

Public Schooling

Education for Democracy

Benjamin R. Barber

It is easy enough to explain the continuing assault on America's children that passes as education policy nowadays: kids are politically invisible—without significant power—and their public schools are no longer regarded as "ours" because they are predominantly nonwhite, peopled by the "invisible children" of the Invisible Man. Even so, putting the moral issues aside, it is hard to comprehend how a tough-minded, realist nation can be so shortsighted. The alternatives to focusing on schools are so much more costly—and grim.

Texas skimps on education but passes a billion-dollar prison bond issue.[1] California, which in 1980 spent roughly four dollars on education for every dollar it spent on jails, today matches every education dollar with a prison dollar. Yet nearly 85 percent of the prison population consists of school dropouts, and it costs three or four times as much to keep the young in prison as it does to keep them in school. It has almost become a cliché to note that one out of three young African American men is either under indictment, in jail, or on parole and that more such young men are serving time in jail than are in college.[2]

Although a fifth to a quarter of all children under six and more than half of minority children live in poverty,[3] everything from school lunches to after-school programs is being slashed at the federal and state levels. Legislators take aim at government budgets, saying they want to spare the next generation the burden of an elephantine deficit, and then shoot down the very programs on which that next generation depends for its education and growth. There is nothing sadder than a country that turns its back on its children, for in doing so it turns away from its own future. How can a nation that has universities and graduate schools that are the envy of the educated world have public primary schools so wretched and inefficient?

If schools are the neglected forges of our future, they are also the abandoned workshops of our democracy. In attacking not just education but *public* education, critics are attacking the very foundation of our democratic civic culture. Public schools are not merely schools *for* the public, but schools of publicness: institutions where we learn what it means to *be* a public and start down the road toward common national and civic identity. They are the forges of our citizenship and the bedrock of our democracy. Yet we seem as a nation to want to disown them. As walls go down elsewhere, they are being raised here by a politics of fear and resentment that fences off cities from suburbs, blacks from whites, poor from rich, and public from private—where, however, *public* means impoverished, dangerous, squalid, and crime prone, and *private* means privileged, safe, wealthy, and secure. But like the walls that were once built into the *Titanic*'s superstructure to create a series of watertight compartments that would make that great ocean liner "unsinkable," the social walls we are erecting today will not save our ship of state. The "*Titanic* mentality" that drives us to compartmentalize our society cannot succeed. We stay afloat only if we recognize that we are all aboard a single ship.

Vilifying public school teachers and administrators and cutting public school budgets even as we subsidize private educational opportunity put us in double jeopardy: for as we put our children at risk, we undermine our common future; at the same moment, in constraining the conditions of liberty for some, we undermine the future of democracy for all. I want here to deal with both sides of the argument: first to suggest that the debate about money is a diversion that exposes our children and our schools to disaster, and second to argue that the fiscal debate completely neglects the vital civic mission of public education.

Let me start with the argument about funding. It has become fashionable to deny that there is any correlation between monies expended and educational results. Comparisons are drawn to parochial schools, charter schools, and private schools where fewer bucks produce a bigger pedagogical bang. "You can't just throw money at the schools and think you can buy better education," say politicians who have been throwing money at national defense, space programs, farm and corporate subsidies, and programs for the elderly for half a century. Three errors mar their argument and the data on which the argument is based:

1. In many municipalities, schools have become the sole surviving *public* institutions and consequently have been burdened with responsibilities far beyond traditional schooling. Schools are now medical clinics, counseling centers, vocational training institutes, police and security outposts, drug rehabilitation clinics, special education centers, and city shelters. They have to act both as sanctuaries from anarchic inner cities and as special social service centers to address all the problems inner cities breed. Compare the budget portion going to conventional classroom education in public schools to the money spent in private schools, and public schools look rather more efficient. But if we ask them to be all-purpose social service centers in an era when social service budgets are being slashed and public schools must operate under such oppressive circumstances, they can only seem inefficient as compared with sleek, single-mission, no-problem-students private schools.

When Kansas City blew (as the critics put it) more than a billion dollars without showing demonstrable improvements in children's test scores, these critics scoffed that it had once again proved that money solves nothing.[4] But Kansas City spent a third of its court windfall on physical improvements (repairing a roof keeps kids dry; it does not in itself improve their reading scores!); another third on court-mandated busing and transportation costs (busing gets kids to a decent school but does not teach them math—indeed, it makes for a longer and more arduous school day); and additional funds went to structural and administrative changes. Less than a quarter of the much-vaunted billion-plus went toward schooling in the narrow sense. And it is far too soon to tell whether this much-smaller sum devoted to education can pay off.

2. Among the costs of public schools that are most burdensome are those that go for special education, discipline, and special services to children who would simply be expelled from (or never admitted into) private and parochial schools or who would be turned over to the appropriate social service agencies (which themselves are no longer funded in many cities). It is the glory and the burden of public schools that they cater to *all* of our children, whether delinquent or obedient, drug-damaged or clean, brilliant or handicapped, privileged or scarred. That is what makes them *public* schools. Elective schemes rooted in vouchers and private screening (parent choice and school selection) assure that only the easily educable and well motivated and parent-supported are in the classroom. A "good school" generally turns out to be a school that good students (made so by previous circumstances and education) attend.[5] Choate and Harvard begin with the very best students: of course they are among the very best schools. Send Choate's pupils to P.S. 31 and watch it become the best public school in America—except (Catch-22) it will no longer be a public school!

3. Our public schools are our point institutions in dealing with our nation's oldest and most intractable problem: racism. As Benjamin DeMott argues in his incisive book, *The Trouble with Friendship*, race in America takes the form of a "caste-like stratification," whose damage can take not months or years but generations to undo. DeMott estimates that only after three generations of relative success is a family previously caught up in the caste of race likely to emerge into something resembling normal, middle-class existence.[6] Minority test scores in a recent experiment were shown to be deeply skewed by what we might call caste awareness of competition with whites—dropping by 10 or 15 percent when

test-takers were told it was a "test." In informal, nontest circumstances, scores were far better. Self-fulfilling prophecy? Living up to expectations for a certain caste? DeMott believes so.

With America divided more completely than ever into Gunnar Myrdal's, the Kerner Commission's, and Andrew Hacker's "two nations"—unequal and hostile—and with public schools more and more acting as the public institutions of last resort for the nation of African Americans (and for nonwhite immigrants), can anyone really expect that dollars spent on their schools will pay off in the same fashion or with the same speed that dollars in privileged private schools do?

We might add to these three sets of issues a more general caveat: why is efficiency so crucial an issue in the public education domain? Will anyone claim that defense dollars are all efficiently expended? Star Wars monies? Space race bucks? Agricultural subsidies? Even in this era of belt-tightening and ideological budget-slashing, Congress has seen fit to raise the defense budget and to put Star Wars back on the nation's agenda on the theory that enough is never enough when it comes to an issue as vital as national security. Will dollars alone buy the most efficient army? An impervious missile defense? Of course not. It takes ingenuity, leadership, and smart ideas, too. But without dollars, you cannot even get started. And in any case, the silent subtext reads, what is a little waste when we are talking about national security?

This is another way to make the point that if you want to see what a nation really values, read the subtext: find out what it is willing to waste money on. Star Wars weapons systems? Tobacco subsidies? Nuclear submarines? There is no limit to waste and inefficiency here. But for schools? Overspend $3.75 and the cost accountants are at the door screaming bloody murder. Norman Mailer tells the story of an interview with a welfare mother back in the sixties when he was running for mayor of New York, just at the moment when the Great Society was beginning to receive criticism for the supposed wastefulness of its inner-city antipoverty programs. The interview concluded almost before Mailer could get it under way when the woman on welfare shouted: "Where is *our* piece of the waste? We want our waste, too!"

Presume the worst about waste in the schools: why is it that education is monitored for every cent budgeted while defense and market subsidies and benefits to the elderly and a host of other programs that have a priority status in America escape even a cursory glance by the fiscal obsessives and ideological accountants? Why are benefits for the elderly entitlements while educational spending on the young is discretionary? Can it be that the children are just not entitled? Are not worth either spending money on or wasting money on? Can it perhaps be that when it comes to kids, spending is in fact itself seen as wasting, because kids belong to a discretionary and disposable generation?

I do not, however, want to leave the argument as one concerned exclusively with issues of spending equality and fiscal efficiency. In fighting to maintain the quality of three-Rs education and the kinds of vocational training that keep our workers competitive in an economy increasingly dominated by global markets and what Robert Reich has called "symbolic analysts,"[7] we need to recall that education also has a central *civic* mission. Our schools are public not just in that they must educate everyone, but in that they must turn a host of "everyones" into something like a single national One: the civic entity that we call a "public." In teaching the public, schools teach what the word *public* means and make possible common ground, public goods, and a sense of the public weal. Public schooling and the public weal are intimately bound together.

When Thomas Jefferson came to consider what he would like to have inscribed on his tombstone, he omitted all mention of his two-term presidency, his acquisition of the Louisiana Territory, his founding of the Democratic Party, and his other great political achievements. Instead, he memorialized only three crucial (to him) features of his biography: his authorship of the Declaration of Independence, his writing of the Virginia Statute of Religious Freedom, and his founding of the University of Virginia. Without public education for all citizens, Jefferson did not see how there could be a democratic politics at all. Without citizens there could be no republic, and without education there could be no citizens.

In joining the Declaration of Independence and the Virginia statute with the founding of the University of Virginia, Jefferson's epitaph disclosed a hidden logic that linked rights to responsibilities, and American independence and democratic self-sufficiency with an educated citizenry. If there was to be a common American people capable of pursuing a common American good in the name of its natural rights, there had to be common schools. Although he boasted in the Declaration of Independence that men were "born free," Jefferson knew well enough that liberty is acquired and that citizens are educated to a responsibility that comes to no man or woman naturally. Without citizens, democracy is a hollow shell. Without public schools, there can be no citizens.

This is a strain of thought that persisted from America's colonial days (when John Adams of Massachusetts boasted that the Commonwealth's schools tutored every young man in citizenship with a ubiquity that put "literate" England to shame) down through the nineteenth century. Tocqueville spoke movingly of the need in democracies for an "apprenticeship of liberty"—what he deemed the most arduous of all apprenticeships.[8] The Common School Movement informed our nineteenth-century educational practices with a sense of civic mission that left no school or college untouched. Not just the land-grant colleges, but nearly every higher educational institution founded in the eighteenth and nineteenth centuries—religious as well as secular, private no less than public—counted among its leading founding principles a dedication to training competent and responsible citizens. Rights were understood to be tied to responsibilities, the freedom to live well and prosper was seen as a product of civic obligations discharged with vigor, and the security of the private sector was thought to depend on the robustness of the public sector.

Sometime toward the end of the last century, with the professionalization of higher education that came to American shores with the German research university model (after which Johns

Hopkins was patterned), schools began to move away from their civic responsibilities. By the end of World War II, higher education had begun to professionalize and vocationalize and specialize in a manner that occluded its civic and democratic mission. Rights and responsibilities were decoupled, and citizenship was relegated to the occasional boring civics lecture—usually a harangue monumentalizing a mythical founding and a set of stereotypical heroes from George Washington to Abraham Lincoln, with whom (at least as they were presented) the increasingly nonwhite population of public schools could have little sense of common cause. So far had rights wandered from responsibilities that young people who explicitly professed that they cherished the system of trial by jury nonetheless argued that no one should be required to do jury service. And the citizen army of conscripts gave way to the volunteer army made up at least in part of those individuals, black and white, for whom society offered few other opportunities.

If our nation is to repossess its civic soul, it needs to recapture the central civic responsibilities of public schools—indeed of schooling in general, K–12 and university, public and private. This means that if American schools are to be defined by the search for literacy, then civic literacy must take its place alongside science, math, English, and cultural literacy. It means that if education is to support school-to-work initiatives that adapt pedagogy to the needs of the workplace, it must also support school-to-citizen initiatives that adapt pedagogy to the needs of the public square—the civic marketplace of civil society. Lawyers and doctors are no more likely to make good citizens than dropouts if their training is limited to the narrow and self-interested world defined by vocational preparation and professional instruction. Youngsters preparing to turn their schooling to the purposes of economic competition with Japan and Germany must also be able to turn their schooling to the purposes of civic cooperation with their fellow Americans in making democracy work.

To rejoin education and liberal citizenship requires only that we take liberal education seriously. Liberal arts education and civic education share a curriculum of critical reflection and autonomous thought. That is how the liberal arts emerged in the modern era in contrast to the feudal servile arts. The latter was job training for the unfree and indentured, and it subordinated learning to an apprenticeship in the vocations; the former devoted itself to free thought and what Tocqueville called "the apprenticeship of liberty." In feudal times, the liberal arts were intended to serve that small minority lucky enough to be born "freemen." If schooling is to be guided once again by its democratic mission, it needs not only to be supported financially, but reendowed with a sense of civic passion. This means that:

- Public schools must be understood as public not simply because they serve the public, but because they establish us as a public. Too much market ideology has left our private and public worlds all topsy-turvy. We have made Madonna's private parts public at the very moment we are demanding, via vouchers, that our last genuinely public institutions be made private. We need incentives to draw parents back into public schools, not vouchers to lure them out. We need to fix, not abandon, those inner-city schools that work least well.
- The *public* in public schools stands for plurality and diversity. America is not a private club defined by one group's historical hegemony. Consequently, multicultural education is not discretionary: it defines demographic and pedagogical necessity. For example, if we want youngsters from Los Angeles whose families collectively speak over 160 languages to be "Americans," we must first acknowledge their diversity and honor their distinctiveness. English will thrive as the first language of America only when those for whom it is a second language feel safe enough in their own language and culture to venture into and participate in the dominant culture. What we share in common is precisely our respect for difference: that is the secret to our strength as a nation, and it is the key to democratic education.
- Schools need to be as democratic as the civic ideals they wish to teach, consistent with the authority of sound pedagogy. This

suggests cooperative learning where those who find the work easy help those who have more difficulty, to the benefit of both, in place of either tracking, by which the quick advance at the expense of the slow, or large, understaffed, detracked classes where the slow advance at the expense of the quick. The goal is not to level down but to secure an aristocracy of everyone in which excellence is the common denominator. This suggests systems of secondary and higher education that provide a role for students in governance and administration. To be sure, students are a transient constituency, and there are issues of hiring, curriculum, and peer review in which their role should necessarily remain extremely limited. But there are other domains where their participation, minimally on a consultative basis, is not only feasible but beneficial to the children and to their educational institutions. Simultaneously, such participation models the kind of democratic culture we presumably wish to teach.

- Learning, above all civic learning, needs to be experiential as well as cognitive. Serving others is not just a form of do-goodism or feel-goodism; it is a road to social responsibility and citizenship. When linked closely to classroom learning ("education-based community service"), it offers an ideal setting for bridging the gap between the classroom and the street, between the theory of democracy and its much more obstreperous practice. Our schools and colleges are not social agencies but teaching and learning communities. Service is an instrument of civic pedagogy. It is a response to William James's quest for a "moral equivalent of war": in serving community, the young forge commonality; in acknowledging difference, they bridge division; in assuming individual responsibility, they nurture social citizenship.
- If it is to serve democratic education, service learning must be a responsibility of everyone, not just a requirement for the criminal or the needy. Teaching the young that white-collar felons or blue-collar loan-seekers owe their country civic service while the well-off and wealthy do not is a poor way to inculcate the ideals of civic equality. Service is a universal entailment of what it means to live in and enjoy the rights of a free society. Loans for those who

need them ought to be offered as a reciprocal right of good citizens, a consequence rather than a prerequisite of citizenship. This is the justification for the vital link that the Corporation for National and Community Service has established between education vouchers and community service.

These revisions of the mission of education, aside from their possible impact on democracy, potentially have a crucial political payoff: they make schools more relevant to the needs of society generally and more pertinent to the concerns of citizens without school-aged children. They thus offer burdened taxpayers reasons why they should support the flow of tax dollars to education. Polls show again and again that citizens object not so much to paying taxes but to the perceived lack of impact of the taxes they pay. They seek not so much lower tax rates but higher payoffs—better results. That our schools are committed not just to educating our children but preparing them to take responsibility for preserving and extending our democracy may make them look like a better bargain.

The rights and freedoms of all Americans depend on the survival of democracy. There is only one road to democracy: education. And in a democracy where freedom comes first—educators and politicians alike take notice—the first priority of education must be the apprenticeship of liberty. Tie every school reform to this principle, and not only education but democracy itself will flourish. Let schools sink further into poverty and privatization, and we will not only put our children at risk but are likely to imperil the very foundation of their liberties and our own.

Notes

1. Scott Pendleton, "Texas Voters Say 'Yea' to More Jail Space," *Christian Science Monitor*, 4 November 1993, p. 2.
2. See, for example, Jocelyn Y. Stewart, "A Bleak Cycle," *Los Angeles Times*, 11 February 1993, pp. E1, E8; Fox Butterfield, "More Blacks in Their 20's Have Trouble With the Law," *New York Times*, 14 June 1995, p. A18; and Ronald Brownstein,

"Why Are So Many Black Men in Jail? Numbers in Debate Equal a Paradox," *Los Angeles Times*, 6 November 1995, p. A5.

3. "4 Million Children Said to Live in 'Distress,'" *New York Times*, 25 April 1994, p. B10; and "Poverty Figures" (Editorial), *Washington Post*, 9 October 1995, p. A26.
4. Of the many reports on Kansas City's efforts to desegregate and improve its schools, see Dennis Farney, "Can Big Money Fix Urban School Systems? A Test Is Under Way," *Wall Street Journal*, 7 January 1992, pp. A1, A4; Dirk Johnson, "Kansas City Uncertain on Its Schools' Fate," *New York Times*, 14 June 1995, p. A17; and Dennis Farney, "Fading Dream? Integration Is Faltering In Kansas City Schools as Priorities Change," *Wall Street Journal*, 26 September 1995, pp. A1, A8.
5. A point made three decades ago in the famous "Coleman Report": James S. Coleman and others, *Equality of Educational Opportunity* (Washington, D.C.: U.S. Government Printing Office, 1966).
6. Benjamin DeMott, *The Trouble with Friendship: Why Americans Can't Think Straight About Race* (New York: Atlantic Monthly Press, 1995), chaps. 4–6, esp. pp. 93–94.
7. Robert B. Reich, *The Work of Nations: Preparing Ourselves for 21st Century Capitalism* (New York: Knopf, 1991).
8. Alexis de Tocqueville, *Democracy in America*, Henry Reeve, trans., Francis Bowen, rev., vol. 1 (1835, 1840; reprint New York: Vintage Books, 1990), p. 247.

Chapter Two

The Meanings of "Public Education"

Theodore R. Sizer

Public education. These are familiar words, so familiar that they slide off American tongues with little argument. We all suppose that everyone knows precisely what they mean. The two words are important. They merit continual definition. The actions practiced in their name deserve fresh attention. Americans in fact do not agree on their meaning.

Public

For most of us the word *public* clearly implies *access*. A public school is one that takes in all comers, just as public transportation takes on all riders. American educational practice, however, generally restricts access, usually on the basis of geography. You go to school in your district, or you go to a magnet school on the basis of entrance requirements. You cannot go to any public school that you might like to attend.

In this respect educational practice is different from public transport. I can take the A7-North or C17-West train on the basis of my need. I live in the city but travel to work in the suburbs, and the suburban transit authority takes my requirements into consideration. Effective public transit authorities, to the best of their abilities, respond with service that reflects the aggregate of all riders' independent and even serendipitous requirements.

Simply, then, *public* in education actually means *unrestricted access to some schools only*. Public transport operates on different assumptions. The restrictive policy for schoolchildren is argued on the premise that their schools are wisely designed to nurture particular communities, that these communities are reflections of geography (not, say, of particular social or philosophical persuasions), and that the state will determine the boundaries of these communities.

Twentieth-century Americans believe that attendance at public schools must be *compulsory*. This is an extraordinary demand, a paradox that makes a point about democracy: all *must* attend school in order that a free society may function. Thus public education is accepted as a universal enterprise. No one is exempt from the schools either operated by the state or, in the case of nonpublic schools and arranged home schooling, endorsed by the state. No one of a certain age can run free in the streets or vegetate in front of the television, at least for seven hours a day, one hundred and eighty days a year. *Public* in this case means that everyone of a certain age must do something in a school building. Here, then, is a public demand for universal behavior.

Freedom remains an option for children younger than five or six (depending on each state's laws) and for everyone over the age of sixteen (or eighteen, again depending on a state's laws). The point of compulsory schooling laws is not that children learn; it is that they attend. The ages within which schooling is required are arbitrary, the result of custom rather than of science. In the late twentieth century, going to school when one is out of diapers and until one is eighteen is what young people do.

This is a *public* demand, argued on the basis that a democracy requires an informed citizenry and that a modern economy demands a skilled workforce. The assumption is that schools will provide citizens and workers. There is no specific expectation—at least until very recent times—that each young citizen will display his or her mastery of these two objectives before leaving the required shelter of public education or that a school has organized itself effectively precisely to teach toward them. The state trusts the schools to meet its standard—which is perhaps the better part of valor as Americans often disagree as to just what is meant by "citizenship education" and even "preparation for employment."

For many, *public* also implies full tax support, that the educational services are free of specific charge. There is no tuition. Some schools charge fees for special services, such as extracurricular programs. Lunch (and sometimes breakfast) is available, for a small charge or free if the youngster comes from a family unable to pay the fee.

However, if a family would prefer its children to go to a school in another district, its members almost always have to move to that district. If real estate prices are high in that new district, the move carries with it a significant cost or is not possible at all. Money shapes the student composition of most public schools, not because the schools' services are not free but because one may have to pay an often substantial premium (in the form of investment in real estate) to join the community that a desired school restrictively serves. Family wealth thus controls access to "public" schools.

For many, the *public* in education implies public management. Public schools are run by administrations selected and overseen by elected or politically appointed school authorities. These administrations are strictly accountable to specific and detailed regulation and direction. That is, the people directly manage their schools. The public are the stockholders that management and directors (that is, the school boards) must satisfy, and, while efficient operation is expected, a profit—that is, a gain in terms other than the children's welfare—is not.

Public transit may or may not have public management. That is, the public interest (it is implied) can at times be served as well or better by independent administration of buses, trolleys, taxis, and trains. The costs of public safety at a national level—national defense—are also largely distributed this way. General Dynamics, for example, is a private company with which federal authorities contract. And in education, especially higher and special education, there are myriad independent organizations that provide a public service at public expense.

In sum, American practice in general implies that a public service can be properly performed by an authority independent of elected officials. Public education at the elementary and secondary level is the country's most significant exception to this rule.

Education

Education for Americans usually means the provision of schools. The contract the state makes with its citizens is that there will be a seat in a classroom somewhere for every child. While there has been some pressure, particularly in recent years, for insisting that each such child delivers something on that investment to some reasonable standard, the overwhelming attention of governing bodies is for the simple provision of places in classrooms. Going to school is the bottom line. Knowing something for that experience is hoped for but—if one carefully follows the way public authorities invest their money and energy—that intent appears far less critical than for the student merely to show up.

Children are typically, and at best, in school some one-third of their waking and discretionary hours per year. That is, the time available for receptive learning is far greater beyond school than within it.

Education, therefore, is much more than classroom seat time. How do young Americans learn? The evidence is substantial that they learn from many sources—their families, peers, the street, the media, school. America is today as never before a culture awash in information and instant images coming insistently from across the globe.

Traditionally, Americans have yielded responsibility for before- and after-school time to families, neighborhoods, and the employers of young people. The record here is clearest in traditional agricultural communities, where youngsters were needed at certain times to help with farm chores.

Americans have, save at the margins, yielded the media to commercial interests. That is, the nonschool education of the child is considered largely beyond the reach of the public interest in education.

Public education as a practical matter in America is operationally (and politically) thus considered in fact the same as *public schooling*, even though young Americans likely learn as much or more of real importance beyond their classrooms as within them.

Public Education

Public education must be recaptured as an idea, indeed an American ideal. It deserves better than to be reduced merely to the provision of a service—maintaining schools—however worthy that service might be.

The nub of it all, ultimately, is just what the public (if it has or can have a coherent voice) wants from public education. Four ends are familiar and to some extent are contradictory.

First, schools serve a *civic function*, providing thereby a "balance-wheel" of democracy, as Horace Mann put it in 1848, in his twelfth annual report to the Massachusetts Board of Education. That is, the common schools are to prepare a people that understands the need for and the working of a civil society.

Second, schools serve an *economic function*, preparing an adequate and dutiful workforce. That is, young people should have at the least the language and mathematical skills necessary to proceed with a job and an understanding of what it means in respect and honesty to provide labor for another.

Third, schools provide *cultivation*, welcoming young people into the best of the culture of the people. The function served here is both personal (the child learns the joy of expression, for its own sake) and collective (a cultivated citizenry is a deeper and thus more compassionate and empathic one).

And fourth, schools provide individuals with the *intellectual strength* to be able to make up their own minds, to stand against false persuasions, and to unleash their idiosyncratic imaginations.

These are reasonable expectations—given our belief in the meaning of an American public education. Each of these expectations has a substantial history. And each, in our day, is riven with disagreement.

There is disagreement on what is meant by a civil society. Is it one in which the people collectively (the state) decide what is right or wrong (what, say, constitutes unacceptable violence—on the hockey rink, in the boxing ring, or on the street; or what constitutes life in the case of an unborn fetus)? What is proper freedom for some is license to others. Freedom is the heart of American civic belief.

Some believe that the schools should train workers at public expense. Others believe that in a capitalist economy such training is the responsibility of employers. Yet others believe that training for jobs as they currently exist skews public education toward the economy as it currently is, underrating the need to educate young people to question conventional definitions of work and to be their own employers.

Some believe that *cultivation*—the inculcation of values—is the responsibility of families and not the duty of the state's schools. They believe that schools should teach basic skills and facts and not more subjective and personal ways of knowing. The opinions that children develop should be shaped at home. Others argue that it is impossible to operate "value free" schools and that no child should be wholly the creature of his or her family. These people argue that the community at large has a proper claim on a child's cultivation, especially when it involves that child's eventual civic duties.

Some believe that the state has no right to help students to think on their own, that such a skill must remain within the family. An attitude of skepticism on the part of adolescents frightens many citizens. Others disagree: respectful skepticism is a staple of serious scholarship and an American practice of long standing. Indeed, the deliberate separation of powers in the Constitution reflected the framers' skepticism about the dependability of a unitary authority.

All of these issues bear on what lies ahead for American public education. Each has been argued separately and vehemently for many years. All must be brought together, the claims of each assessed, and a new, clearer conception of public education ultimately described.

Public education is in our time under heroic siege. The schools are profoundly segregated by social class, and thus in many communities by race and ethnicity. The "melting pot" common school is rare. Further, the monies supporting the schools serving poorer communities are scarcer than those serving the wealthier. One sees regularly the juxtaposition within but a few miles of forlorn schools, poorly equipped and housed, and places dazzling with facilities and opportunities. No major industrial nation tolerates such inequities at the scale that does America.

Government bureaucracies have substantial control over the schools, and the various political estates—the school boards, the state boards, the unions, among others—in many communities, especially the big cities, have drifted into gridlock, causing any significant reform to be ferociously difficult to carry out. Key policies are often set and administered by bodies that are at a great distance from the communities and highly unlikely, therefore, to be accountable to the particular people most affected by the quality of public education: the families of school-aged children. Accordingly, they can act—and unfortunately do often act—with impunity, ignoring, for example, the stunning inequities within the system.

There are no standards to the system: just running it is apparently enough. Political leaders thunder about standards for the children and their schools, but their silence on standards for themselves is virtually universal. Leaders far from the schools can demand that high-quality work be done by the teachers and students (say, in science) without taking care that the conditions for that work—good laboratories, well-stocked libraries, appropriate student loads per teacher, adequate time—are available. This hypocrisy is so prevalent that it is barely recognized.

The media, that extraordinary teacher, is removed in public policy from education. Policies for its use reflect virtually no attention to its impact on children. And as technology's power increases with the computer revolution, the distance between the rich and the poor increases. Richer folks can afford PCs and access to the Internet. Poorer folks cannot. As the possibilities for home schooling rapidly increase thanks to technology, the glaring discrepancies between social classes widen once again. And the nation is further robbed of the talent residing in its low-income communities.

Public education is an idea, not a mechanism. It promises every young citizen a fair grounding in the intellectual and civic tools necessary to have a decent life in this culture and economy. It promises the rest of us that the rising generations have the tools to keep America a place worthy of residence. It signals that we are one—*e pluribus unum*.

We fall lamentably short of that goal today. It is one of America's greatest and most wounding embarrassments.

Chapter Three

Education, Equity, and the Right to Learn

Linda Darling-Hammond

Public education is central to the promise of American democracy. In the birthing of America, in the great debates over whether a people could create and sustain a truly democratic rule, Alexander Hamilton offered this argument for a representative rather than a popular democratic form of government: "Thy people," he told Thomas Jefferson, "are a beast." Hamilton's lack of faith in the ability of the people to make sound decisions about their own lives and those of their communities—a lack of faith that was widely shared then and, we might note, now as well—was the basis for proposals that this new nation should be governed by elites on behalf of the people, who could not be trusted to govern themselves.

Thus challenged, Jefferson argued that "the people" could be prepared to govern responsibly through a system of public education that would develop an intelligent populace and support a popular intelligence. Public schools—which would prepare citizens to debate and decide among competing ideas, to weigh the individual and the common good, and to make judgments that could sustain democratic institutions and ideals—would enable the people to make sound decisions and withstand the threat of tyranny.

Jefferson's argument and our democracy rest on a kind of schooling that goes beyond "basic skills" or literacy. To ensure a populace capable of democratic decision making, schools must cultivate in all students the skills, knowledge, and understanding that both arm them with a keen intelligence capable of free thought and lead them to embrace the values undergirding our pluralistic democracy—that, in other words, enable them to live productively together. Jefferson's ideal was the kind of education W.E.B. DuBois described in the darkening days of the early McCarthy era:

> Of all the civil rights for which the world has struggled and fought for 5,000 years, the right to learn is undoubtedly the most fundamental. . . . The freedom to learn, curtailed even as it is today, has been bought by bitter sacrifice. And whatever we may think of the curtailment of other civil rights, we should fight to the last ditch to keep open the right to learn, the right to have examined in our schools not only what we believe, but what we do not believe; not only what our leaders say, but what the leaders of other groups and nations, and the leaders of other centuries have said. We must insist upon this to give our children the fairness of a start which will equip them with such an array of facts and such an attitude toward truth that they can have a real chance to judge what the world is and what its greater minds have thought it might be.[1]

Public education is central to the promise of American democracy in another way as well: it provides a vehicle for all citizens, regardless of wealth or circumstances of birth, to aspire to the rights and benefits of this society and to create a community with shared purpose. Education for democracy must educate us not only for economic fitness or for the ability to make decisions in a voting booth, but also for a shared social life and the pursuit of human possibility. Democracy cannot be sustained if its members do not connect with one another in productive ways. Democratic education is the kind of education that, as Maxine Greene puts it, allows people to "act together to give freedom a concrete existence in their lives"—a freedom that is made possible "only when people come together with some common notion of personal integrity . . . in a life consciously lived in common."[2] Thus, individual and collective freedom are inextricably intertwined.

These are especially critical times for democratic education. As the twenty-first century nears, most nations around the world are seeking to transform their education systems to respond to changing economic, demographic, political, and social imperatives. Nearly all countries are engaged in school reform aimed at much higher levels of education for much greater numbers of citizens—a demand created by a new information age, major economic shifts, and a resurgence of democracy around the globe. In the United States, as elsewhere, efforts to rethink schooling have been stimulated by the need to prepare a much more diverse and inclusive group of future citizens and workers to manage complexity, find and use new resources and technologies, and work cooperatively to frame and solve novel problems.

We have entered an era in which all people must learn flexibly and effectively to survive and succeed in a fast-changing world. If we cannot accomplish this task at this moment in history, a deeply stratified society—one divided by access to knowledge and the opportunity to learn—is likely to undo our chances for democratic life and government. These changes define a new mission for education and for teaching: one that requires schools not merely to deliver instructional services but to ensure that all students actually learn. This kind of education requires teachers not merely to cover the curriculum but to enable diverse learners to construct their own knowledge and develop their talents in effective and powerful ways.

Right now our democracy is in trouble. Only about one-third of our citizens feel sufficiently interested or empowered to participate in a regular way in the political process. Racial, ethnic, and class divisions are growing as confusion about vast social changes creates a search for scapegoats. The ability of citizens to come together for positive social action in their local communities seems undermined by a combination of intergroup antagonism and a sense of cynicism and hopelessness about the usefulness of collective effort. Meanwhile, dramatically unequal access to education and employment routinely and systematically disadvantages low-income students and students of color and results in growing rates of crime, incarceration, structural unemployment, homelessness, drug use, and social dysfunction. These conditions increasingly victimize those trapped in a growing underclass, as well as all of those who pay—financially and socially—for its costs to the broader society. In many and growing ways, unequal access to the kind of education needed to sustain a democracy threatens the very foundations of our nation.

It might be argued that social and political participation is a goal that goes beyond what schools can influence or should be concerned about. Indeed most debates about schools and most efforts to reform them focus nearly exclusively on how they will train future workers so as to maintain particular views of what will produce a healthy economy. Yet if we do not educate in ways that enable people to participate actively in an inclusive social and political life, serious social dysfunctions will undermine our economic advances. A key function of public education is to form a public that can talk, work, and make decisions together. This function is frequently forgotten or subsumed to industrial goals for schooling. At times, economic objectives for schools conflict directly with a productive and inclusive social education. For example, efforts to prepare workers for a factory economy led to forms of schooling that reinforced passivity and compliance rather than independent thinking and that created stratification among classes of people. These efforts left many citizens without the tools needed for collective discourse and action in a healthy democracy.

Democratic life requires access to forms of knowledge that enable creative life and thought as well as access to a social dialogue that enables democratic communication and participation. Growing up a humane and decent people who can appreciate others and take satisfaction in doing things well requires schools that allow for humanity and decency, that cultivate appreciation, that create social community, and that support deep learning about things that matter to the people in them. For all the other purposes of schooling, education is a source of nurturance for the spirit, although it can be, and too often is, conducted in a way that deadens and demoralizes. Schooling, managed as a tedious and coercive activity, can create frustrations that emerge sooner or later in self-deprecation or cruelty to others. However, where a real connection is made between students and teachers in the pursuit of meaningful accomplishments, possibilities for developing lifelong capacities for learning, doing, and relating to others are greatly expanded.

A democratic education should enable all people to find out and act on who they are, what their passions, gifts, and talents may be, what they care about, and how they want to make a contribution to each other and the world. It is an education that is profoundly social, one that, as John Dewey suggested, enables a person not just to be good but to "be good for something"—and that something is the "capacity to live as a social member so that what he gets from living with others balances with what he contributes. What he gets and gives as a human being, a being with desires, emotions, and ideas, is not external possessions, but a widening and deepening of conscious life—a more intense, disciplined, and expanding realization of meanings."[3]

Unfortunately, the bureaucratic school created at the turn of the twentieth century was not organized to meet these needs for intellectual, social, or personal development. Its mission was not to educate all students well but to process a great many efficiently, selecting and supporting only a few for "thinking work." Strategies for sorting and tracking students were developed to ration the scarce resources of expert teachers and rich curriculum and to justify the standardization of teaching procedures within groups. This, in turn, enabled greater routinization of teaching and less reliance on professional judgment, a corollary of the nineteenth-century decision to structure teaching as semiskilled work. Bureaucracy also traded off teacher, parent, and student participation in decision making for the presumed efficiencies of predetermined practices, thus excluding school members from discussion of and decisions about what education is and what it should be.

Like early twentieth-century manufacturing industries, modern schools were designed as highly specialized, hierarchical organizations—divided into grade levels and subject matter departments, separate tracks, programs, and auxiliary services—each managed separately and run by carefully specified procedures engineered to yield standard products. The search for the "one best system" of schooling[4] was based on the assumptions that students are standardized and that educational treatments can be prescribed and delivered in segmented form; that human behavior can be directed by rules; and that specifying courses, textbooks, testing instruments, and management systems would lead to student learning.

For the masses of students, the goal was simple and straightforward: to instill rudimentary skills and the basic workplace socialization needed to follow orders and conduct prescribed tasks neatly and punctually. The rote learning needed for these early twentieth-century objectives still predominates in today's schools, reinforced by top-down prescriptions for teaching practice, mandated curriculum packages, standardized tests that focus on low cognitive level skills, and continuing underinvestment in teacher knowledge.

The school structures created to implement this conception of teaching and learning are also explicitly impersonal. Students move along a conveyor belt from one teacher to the next, grade to grade, and class period to class period, with little opportunity to become well known over a sustained period of time to any adults who can consider them as whole people or as developing intellects. Secondary school teachers may see 150 or more students a day, unable to come to know any individual student or family well. Teachers work in isolation from one another, stamping students with lessons, with little time to work with others or share their knowledge. Students, too, tend to work alone and passively, listening to lectures, memorizing facts and formulae, and engaging in independent seatwork at their separate desks.

When teachers and students have little opportunity to come to know one another well, and students have little opportunity to relate to any adult in the school on an extended, personal level, it should not be surprising that the cracks into which students can fall become virtual chasms. The alienation many students derive from this experience reduces their opportunities to become well educated and their ability to identify in a positive way with the social structure that is their closest potential connection to society as a whole. Even for those who try to make it work, the fragmented nature of the daily class schedule as well as the relationships that must fit within it tend to reduce learning to the kinds of tasks that are easily bounded, making it more difficult to find room in the schooling process for those intense encounters with ideas and mentors that produce deeper levels of understanding and caring.

The bureaucratic structures for schooling created to batch process masses of students work against democratic goals on many levels: their size and procedures—including the assembly-line movement of students through classes, the lack of long-term personal relationships among adults and students, rigid tracks separating groups of students from one another, and the isolation of teachers—preclude most forms of community building and shared discourse. They not only maintain inequalities in access to knowledge, they also heighten divisions among groups and fail to prepare most young people to become active social participants and leaders. They model and reinforce social stratification rather than inclusiveness, passivity and disengagement rather than active participation, and unthinking acceptance of the knowledge constructed by others rather than critical thought and the development of knowledge.

Education for democracy requires not only experiences that develop serious thinking but also access to social understanding, developed by personal participation in a democratic community and direct experience of multiple perspectives. To accomplish this, schools must enact democracy rather than merely preach about it. In *Democracy and Education*, Dewey stated that "a democracy is more than a form of government; it is primarily a mode of associated living."[5] He stressed the importance of creating circumstances in which people share a growing number of interests and participate in a growing number of associations with other groups, noting that, "In order to have a large number of values in common, all the members of the group must have an equable opportunity to receive and to take from others. There must be a large variety of shared undertakings and experiences. Otherwise, the influences which educate some into masters, educate others into slaves. And the experience of each party loses in meaning, when the free interchange of varying modes of life-experience is arrested."[6]

Finding what we have in common requires that we communicate from the vantage points of our separate, but increasingly related, interests. Each of us has to find a way to express and locate our own experiences in the course of our education in order to connect with new knowledge and with the experiences of others. We also need a way to find and understand the experiences of others so that we can communicate with them in an educative manner. Thus, all of us need a multicultural education to be citizens together.

Far from encouraging separatism, communications about our diverse experiences help us educate each other and ourselves about the connections among our different associations. It is our commitment to communicate about and across our multiple perspectives that is the essence of a democracy and the glue that holds a democratic society together. A communication that is, in Dewey's words, "vitally social, or vitally shared"[7] is one that allows us at least partially to experience the perspectives of another, and by that connection to develop understanding and appreciation for that person's experience and understanding of the world.

These appreciations of other perspectives provide the foundation for a broader *shared* perspective that in turn allows us to form communities and societies. It may seem paradoxical, but it is only by acknowledging the reality and the legitimacy of diverse points of view that we can begin the work of forging a common point of view that takes account of the others. Such an education helps us avoid what Edmund Gordon describes as "communicentric bias: the tendency to make one's own community the center of the universe and the conceptual frame that constrains thought."[8] The ability to appreciate perspectives is an important aspect of both cognitive and social functioning; it is one of Piaget's indicators of higher stages of cognitive development as well as a goal of socially responsive education.

The capacity to achieve associations beyond those of any narrow group—to live and learn heterogeneously together—is required for the development of democracy, for the expansion of knowledge, and for the search for truth. Just as inquiry about important problems must cross departmental boundaries, for the same reasons, such inquiry must also cross community and cultural boundaries. The basis of the very earliest universities was that they tried to bring together scholars from all over the known world. They sought to create ways to share diverse perspectives from various geographic areas, cultures, and disciplines as the basis for developing knowledge and finding truth. The same ideal of knowledge building and truth finding—of looking for powerful, shared ideas to arise from diverse understandings and experiences of the world—undergirds the concept of a democratic, multicultural education that encompasses the many views of its participants—that is, all the views that must be accommodated in the common space of our social life.

Unfortunately, many schools and classrooms, especially those serving less-advantaged students and students in lower tracks, are distinctly nondemocratic in their approaches to teaching and learning: they are characterized by a noninvolving autocratic atmosphere, passive activities, and few opportunities to discuss real questions, work cooperatively, and engage in decision making. Organized for conformity and compliance at the expense of intellectual habits of mind, these classrooms undermine the development of skills needed for enlightened and responsible citizenship—the ability to deliberate, to think critically, to develop and express one's voice articulately so as to participate in the shaping of one's society.[9]

Tracking and unresponsive forms of teaching subvert the purposes of schooling in a democracy by creating unequal classes of citizens, providing only one class with the skills and knowledge necessary for full participation in the society. This jeopardizes the foundations for democracy and prevents students from learning how to engage in the joint construction of community because they are kept separate and disengaged by the structures of schooling. As we reinvent education for the next century, we need schools that are structured for community and for caring as well as for critical thinking.

Recent critiques of bureaucratic schooling, especially the American high school, have noted the dysfunctional consequences of relying on controls, compliance, and coercion to maintain a stratified and dehumanizing organizational structure rather than developing relationships and responsibility as the basis for shared community. Growing research evidence illustrates the success of smaller schools and school units fostering common learning experiences, close faculty and peer relations, cooperative work, and participation of parents, teachers, and students in making decisions.[10] Communitarian models for schooling provide alternatives to the disengagement, separation, and inequality fostered by bureaucratic approaches.

Current school reforms are supporting a growing number of schools in reshaping their curricula, organization patterns, and governance to focus on learning for understanding, a personalized environment, and a collaborative learning community for children and adults. Drawing on a long tradition of progressive education historically available only to the affluent and to those philosophically committed to child-centered approaches, restructured schools aim to educate all children, rather than a small minority, for "thinking work" and to prepare students to become powerful, productive citizens where now so many become alienated and disconnected from school and society instead. This agenda is fundamentally democratic: to join an empowering vision of education to the quest for educational equity by creating humane and intellectually challenging learning environments for children in all communities.

Many such schools have flourished in each era of earlier progressive reforms—at the turn of the century, in the 1930s, and in the 1960s. Fostered by grassroots networks like the Coalition of

Essential Schools, the National Network for Educational Renewal, the School Development Program, and many others, new schools and transformations of existing schools are demonstrating that all students can be well educated in settings structured for caring and for common high standards. They are focusing on more challenging and exciting kinds of learning, helping students to construct, generate, and use their own knowledge. They are creating communities of learners that empower students to seek their own answers and to pose many of their own questions. And they are finding teaching strategies and personalized structures that reach diverse learners more effectively.

The transformation of the American high school may be taking place in Philadelphia's Charter Schools program and the launching of one hundred new, small high schools in New York City, which provide sustained adult-student relationships and a common core curriculum in smaller school settings.[11] Such schools not only provide a more equal education with markedly better outcomes for all of their students, they also respond to students' needs to find places in which their experiences are acknowledged and they can establish strong social connections with others.

Earlier efforts aimed at more learner-centered teaching and more universal, high-quality education were undermined in each of the previous reform eras by underinvestment in teachers and in school capacity. Lawrence Cremin argued that "progressive education . . . demanded infinitely skilled teachers, and it failed because such teachers could not be recruited in sufficient numbers."[12] Because of this failure, in each of its iterations progressivism gave way to standardizing influences: in the efficiency movement of the 1920s, the teacher-proof curriculum reforms of the 1950s, and the back-to-the-basics movement of the 1970s and 1980s. But these attempts at simplifying schooling also failed, leading to renewed criticism of schools and attempts to restructure them.

Current efforts at democratic school reform are likely to last and spread only if they are built on a foundation of teaching knowledge achieved by the creation of a profession of teaching that "completes rather than competes with democracy"[13] and that commits to structural rather than merely symbolic change. This will mean reinventing school organizations so that they can be humane and socially productive, supporting the learning of teachers about how to educate diverse learners in empowering ways, and attending explicitly to the inequalities that threaten to undermine our society as well as our schools. We cannot secure this agenda by privatizing or voucherizing schools to protect the children of the rich in ways that increase their distance from the children of ordinary Americans, or even by restructuring some schools while others continue to function as inhumane, antidemocratic, and unproductive detention centers. We cannot be satisfied to prepare some teachers extraordinarily well while others (who invariably teach the most vulnerable children) are left to flounder, ineffective in the face of the demands that bombard them. We cannot sustain our society if we do not seek to invent systemwide supports for schools that allow for high-quality, intellectually challenging, democratically grounded education for all children.

For those of us engaged in the work of school reform, this agenda calls on us for an even bigger set of commitments than we have ever before been asked to imagine. It calls on suburban educators and citizens to support the equalization of finances for schools in central cities and poor rural areas. It calls on teachers and other educators to develop and support policies that create greater professional accountability for themselves and their colleagues, including assuming collective responsibility for ensuring that those who enter and stay in teaching are committed to students and competent to support their learning. It calls on us to work to surmount the walls that have separated us in our own institutions—across department, division, and union lines. And it calls for all of us to be as concerned with educating policymakers and the public as we are about educating our students. It calls on us to put aside self-interest on behalf of bigger ideals. Can we do this? I believe we can. There are more of us committed to this agenda in more different kinds of communities with more connections to one another than ever before in the history of this nation. Must we do it? Indeed we must if we are to create a public education system that can meet the demands of democracy in this century and in the years beyond.

Notes

1. W.E.B. DuBois, "The Freedom to Learn," in *W.E.B. DuBois Speaks*, ed. Philip S. Foner (New York: Pathfinder, 1970), pp. 230–231.
2. Maxine Greene, *Education, Freedom, and Possibility*. Inaugural Lecture as William F. Russell Professor in the Foundations of Education, Teachers College, Columbia University, 1984, pp. 4, 5.
3. John Dewey, *Democracy and Education* (1916; reprint New York: Free Press, 1966), p. 359.
4. David B. Tyack, *The One Best System: A History of American Urban Education* (Cambridge, Mass.: Harvard University Press, 1974).
5. Dewey, *Democracy and Education*, p. 87.
6. Dewey, *Democracy and Education*, p. 84.
7. Dewey, *Democracy and Education*, p. 6.
8. Edmund W. Gordon, "Coping with Communicentric Bias in Knowledge Production in the Social Sciences," *Educational Researcher* 19 (April 1990): 19.
9. These findings are detailed in Linda Darling-Hammond and Jacqueline Ancess, "Democracy and Access to Knowledge," in *Democracy, Education, and the Schools*, ed. Roger Soder (San Francisco: Jossey-Bass, 1996), pp. 151–81.
10. Valerie Lee, Anthony Bryk, and MaryLou Smith, "The Organization of Effective Secondary Schools," in *Review of Research in Education*, vol. 19, ed. Linda Darling-Hammond (Washington, D.C.: American Educational Research Association, 1993); and Linda Darling-Hammond, Jacqueline Ancess, and Beverly Falk, *Authentic Assessment in Action: Studies of Schools and Students at Work* (New York: Teachers College Press, 1995).

11. Michelle Fine, *Chartering Urban School Reform* (New York: National Center for Restructuring Education, Schools, and Teaching, Teachers College, Columbia University, 1994); and Linda Darling-Hammond and others, *Inching Toward Reform: The Coalition Campus Schools Project* (New York: National Center for Restructuring Education, Schools, and Teaching, Teachers College, Columbia University, in press).
12. Lawrence Cremin, *The Genius of American Education* (New York: Vintage Books, 1965), p. 56.
13. Carl Glickman, Presentation to 4 Seasons Conference, Orlando, Florida, June 1995.

Chapter Four

On Restoring Public and Private Life

Gary D Fenstermacher

For generations Americans lived two lives: one private, the other public. This dual existence was not a sign of some lamentable personality disorder. It was, rather, a condition of health. The private life was lived with loved ones, dear friends, and perhaps one's spiritual guide and confessor. The public life was experienced beyond the home and confessional; it occurred where one was not generally well known save perhaps in a single role, such as teacher, plumber, or attorney. Private life was often composed and frequently genial, consisting as it did of persons bound by blood, love, long periods of shared experience, or an intimate access to God. Public life was not so composed, as it consisted of many different kinds of persons seeking some sort of cooperative existence without benefit of the binding forces of family, love, or religious spirit.

These descriptions are framed in the past tense to alert us to the possibility that the difference between public and private life has disappeared from American culture. For some, including this writer, the disappearance of difference is a bad sign for democracy. For others, as we shall see, it may open newer and more exciting possibilities for life in a democratic society. Before becoming enmeshed in the issues, it would be well to clarify further the notions of *public* and *private*.

As a child, I recall hearing quite often the expression, "Such things are not done in public," or some similarly worded caution. It was usually my mother who said it. But I also recall my father, on hearing one of his children say something troubling, comment with a frown, "I trust that will not become public." At the time, I did not wonder much about these admonitions. I cannot ever recall asking, "What's the public?" Somehow I was aware of what my parents were saying to me. They were telling me that certain behavior is not revealed beyond the threshold of one's home, that the expectations for my conduct changed when I walked out the front door. Thus I came to have a sense that "out there" is different from "in here."

"In here" we talked, though not often and without much detail, about my father's salary and how his income was expended. But that topic was not allowed to be continued "out there." "In here" we discussed sex and intimacy—again not often or in much detail—with the understanding that such talk would not resume when we stepped off the front porch. I recall my mother's enjoyment of off-color, though not vulgar, jokes. She delighted in sharing these with us but would briefly reprove us when we told such jokes to her—this reproof tucked neatly into her laughter just after we delivered the punch line. We spoke, too, of troublesome relatives and exasperating friends, always with the understanding that such talk would never be repeated "out there."

It is of more than passing interest that it was usually my mother who cautioned my brothers and me about the differences between private and public speech and conduct. It is a role mothers played for many generations. The historian Joel Spring points out that "one effect of the American Revolution was to link the domestic responsibilities of women with broader public purposes. . . . Women, as mothers, were seen as having the responsibility for shaping the character of their sons as future republicans."[1] As we shall have occasion to note a bit later, this feature of motherhood provides a provocative point of contrast to the conception of public and private I am describing here. For the moment, however, let us stick to the line of argument with which this chapter began.

As my parents drew the distinction between in here and out there, out there became a quite different place from in here. Out there was a place that called for caution in what one said or did, a place that required a degree of care not needed in here. It was a place where quick judgments were unhelpful and tolerance was needed, because people out there did not know you as well as your family did, and thus were not so likely to understand hastily expressed thoughts or to forgive unkind actions. In here I was known and loved and given great range to explore forms of speech and conduct; out there I was not so well known, and there were far more expectations about how to fit in and act than there were in here.

From the vantage point of a child, out there seemed to have many more rules for participation and called for special kinds of behavior. Such words as *civil*, *propriety*, *credible*, and *decorum* appeared to have far more importance out there than in here. And though we, as children, were taught lessons about fairness, equality, and freedom in here, these words made more sense to us as "out there" words. Other notions, such as compassion, courage, and respect, received attention as "in here" words—although it was expected that we would exhibit such traits on both sides of the threshold.

As I recall these aspects of my childhood, I am struck by their apparent absence from these times. The language of film, video, and popular music seems to carry no distinction between in here and out there, as words once thought unfit for public discourse are now commonly heard. Of course, such language was not thought fit for private discourse either, but it was permitted in that context in ways it was not in public discourse. Visual images of intimate sexual conduct and of hideous violence, once thought so indecent or in such bad taste as to be banned from the public arena, are now an everyday part of that sphere. Civility and decorum seem no longer to be features of the public setting, as automobile drivers exchange once-obscene gestures, magazine advertisements appeal to the prurient or feral sides of human nature, and certain forms of popular music call for disobedience that could not by any stretch be called civil.

As one ponders these cultural transformations, it is relatively easy to surmise that we have lost "out there." There does not appear to be a distinct form of public life in our culture. Instead, our private lives seem to have become our public life. In his *The Fall of Public Man*,[2] Richard Sennett attends in remarkable scholarly detail to this very point. He argues that public life has been corrupted by the private realm. It is as if that which was once private has leaked into that which was once public, producing a kind of corrosion that has as its result the loss of what, in an earlier time, was called the public morality.

The American press certainly seems to think that something of this sort has occurred. The June 12, 1995, cover of *Time* asks in bold letters: "ARE MUSIC AND MOVIES KILLING AMERICA'S SOUL?" A recent *Newsweek* column by Meg Greenfield is called "It's Time for Some Civility."[3] A July 1994 op-ed piece in the *New York Times* carried the title, "The Death of Civility."[4] Syndicated columnist Molly Ivins has written about what she calls the "new incivility."[5] These are but a small sample of recent writing on such related topics as the decline in this nation's moral standards, the lament at the loss of family values, the destruction of the common good, the disappearance of a common language, and the disintegration of a national identity for all Americans.

There seems little doubt that our culture has been transformed. Though I am less sure than Richard Sennett that this transformation comes about through the corruption of the public life by the private, it is clear that whatever the public life of today is, it is not at all like the public life we thought existed prior to, say, World War II. Various scholars have commented on this, calling what we have today "anomic democracy" or "deficit democracy."[6] Television has had an enormous impact on reshaping notions of public life, as have the psychological and spiritual consequences of living in an age when our existence on this planet could be crippled or ended by nuclear madness or careless disregard for the environment.

We have, in comparison to the past, become knife-edged in our discourse, excessively dramatic in our conduct, and indiscriminate in the auditory and visual imagery we employ. There are far fewer controls "out there" to temper speech and deed, and to moderate conflicting views. Political theorist Benjamin Barber notes the importance of civility to the preservation of our democratic way of life when he remarks that "the autonomy and the dignity no less than the rights and freedoms of all Americans depend on the survival of democracy: not just democratic government, but a democratic civil society and a democratic civic culture."[7] Yet civil society and civic culture are in trouble. Jean Bethke Elshtain, another political theorist, contends that "we are in danger of losing democratic civil society. It is that simple and that dangerous, springing, as it does, not from a generous openness to sharp disagreement—democratic feistiness—but from a cynical and resentful closing off of others."[8]

This disintegration of public life suggests a bleak future for the well-being of our nation. To understand why, consider this cogent analysis by the respected philosopher and political theorist, John Rawls: "A modern democratic society is characterized not simply by a pluralism of comprehensive religious, philosophical, and moral doctrines but by a pluralism of incompatible yet reasonable comprehensive doctrines. No one of these doctrines is affirmed by citizens generally. Nor should one expect that in the foreseeable future one of them, or some other reasonable doctrine, will ever be affirmed by all, or nearly all, citizens."[9]

Given this characterization of a modern democratic society, how is such a society ever to work out its differences in the absence of the norms of discourse and participation that were once associated with life in the public context? That is, if we are a nation of "incompatible yet reasonable comprehensive doctrines," how do we establish the common ground upon which we must stand if we are to negotiate our differences in reasonable and peaceful ways?

There have been many arguments of late, Barber's and Elshtain's among them, that we cannot do so without some sense of public, some place in our social lives where civility, decorum, and reasonableness constitute the agreed-upon rules of participation. If there is no longer a public aspect to our social lives, and there is only the private, then it appears that the resolution of problems arising from difference is all the more difficult to achieve—if it is possible at all. Within the private realm, we may feel entitled to our differences without a sense of need to work through what it means to retain these differences within a community, on behalf of the commonweal. In the private realm, we may not only expect to be tolerated for our differences, we may seek to be loved for them, or perhaps in spite of them.

An attitude of this kind bodes ill for a liberal democracy. In a liberal democracy,[10] primacy is awarded to the individual's freedom to pursue his or her own vision of the good life. A government in a liberal democracy is instituted, in part, to ensure that one individual's pursuit of the good life does not unduly restrict another individual's freedom to pursue a different vision of the good life. A government's capacity to achieve a just balance among conflicting pursuits of different individuals or groups of individuals is dependent on some shared, common conception of the point and purpose of human existence within a political boundary (and, increasingly, on the planet as a whole).

Without a public place to carry out the debate on whether your vision of the good and my vision of the good can be achieved without our injuring one another, our differences may readily become occasions for anger, conflict, and perhaps, as we have seen so dramatically in what was once Yugoslavia, armed hostilities of a most brutal and inhuman kind. A *public place* is not merely a geographic location; it is also a set of traits and skills possessed by those who would occupy this place, as well as a shared understanding of what must be common to all if each is to have the greatest possible opportunity to pursue his or her own vision. This sense of what constitutes a public place, as well as its critical importance to democracy, has led a number of scholars to argue for the importance of restoring public life in America. Here public life takes the form of an "out there," as my childhood recollection would frame it, where norms, standards, values, and rules are held in common for the purpose of sustaining a society where each is free to peacefully pursue life, liberty, and happiness to such an extent that someone else's pursuit of these same goods is not unduly curtailed.

Education performs a crucial role in forming this public setting. The norms, standards, values, and rules just mentioned are taught and practiced in the course of gaining an education. Indeed, this point accounts for a democratic nation's compelling interest in education, for it is in a nation's schools that the norms, standards, values, and rules for participation in the public arena are taught and practiced. Historian Robert Westbrook begins a recent essay on public schooling and American democracy with these words: "The relationship between public schooling and democracy is a conceptually tight one."[11] Walter Feinberg, an educational philosopher, contends that "the role of public education is to create and recreate a public by giving voice to an otherwise inarticulate, uninformed mass."[12]

In these times, many educational policymakers and practitioners give little consideration to the critical links between education and democracy.[13] While this nation is in the midst of cultural hurricanes engendered by bitter divisions over race, language, religion, and moral values, educational policymakers force the debate over America's schools into a teapot of comparatively puny issues such as academic standards, measures of academic achievement, and getting all children ready for school (though with hardly a thought to the point and purpose of the school they are presumably getting ready for). In Westbrook's words, "American democracy is now weak and its prospects are dim. The anemia of public life in the United States . . . is reflected in public schooling that, despite lip service to education for democratic citizenship, has devoted few resources or even much thought to its requirements."[14]

The recent work of David Berliner and Bruce Biddle argues that many educational policymakers justify their teapot agenda for the schools with reasons unrelated to the educational benefit of children or the strengthening of democracy. As Berliner and Biddle put it, powerful people are "pursuing a political agenda designed to weaken the nation's public schools, redistribute support for those schools so that privileged students are favored over needy students, or even abolish those schools altogether. To this end, they have been prepared to tell lies, suppress evidence, scapegoat educators, and sow endless confusion."[15] At a time when so many political theorists, philosophers, and historians are issuing warnings about the fragile state of democracy in America, the flummery among educational policymakers must be recognized for being just that. Many theorists argue that the rhetoric of standards, goals, and test scores must be halted in favor of a far more proactive agenda on behalf of a "civil society and civic culture" (to use Barber's words).

Unfortunately, we are not in quite so fine a position for this restorative work as some seem to think. If we merely return to older conceptions of private and public, little ground will have been gained. These older conceptions are freighted with presumptions about the superiority of public life to private life, about the role of women in private and public space, and about whether there are multiple versions of the common good (and, if so, whose version will prevail). For these reasons it is important to reconsider past and current conceptions of private and public, asking whether we can revise them so that they exhibit a better fit with these times. Let us begin with the place of the private in relation to the public.

In the lament over the dissolution of a common and constructive public life in America, we have, perhaps, been too quick either to blame the private realm or to ignore its role in the formation of a healthy public. Sennett's analysis, as well argued as it is, views the private as a kind of ill wind for the public, wherein the quality of public life is diminished by its assuming more the character of private life. This way of framing the problem is rooted in a perspective of the private as something less noble and less important to human attainment than the public. This view of the private may be the legacy of Hannah Arendt's analysis of the public-private distinction as developed in one of her best-known works, *The Human Condition*.[16]

Arendt leads us to a view of the private that is grounded in the household and the oversight of one's property and wealth. As she recounts the conduct of the classical Greeks, the private is a place to be escaped in order to participate in the public realm. On reading Arendt's descriptions of the private and public realms, it is hard to avoid the conclusion that the goodness and nobility of the species is made manifest in the public, not the private, realm.[17]

Although there can be no public without the private, the public is where the grandeur and potential of humankind is situated. Many of today's advocates for the restoration of a healthy, constructive public life appear to hold something of the same views of private and public as Arendt does.

Judith Swanson's insightful analysis of the public and the private in Aristotle's philosophy[18] points us to a very different interpretation. Swanson develops her thesis by using Arendt's analysis of the public and the private as something of a foil. On Swanson's view, Arendt errs in describing Aristotle's conception of the private as something to be escaped in order to experience the freedom and opportunities for virtue that are available only in the polis. For Swanson, the private and the public are much more interactive, and far more interdependent, than Arendt portrays them to be. Swanson argues that the public sphere has a responsibility to nurture the private sphere, for it is in the private sphere that so many of the virtues needed for effective participation in the polis are developed. It is particularly in the rearing of children, in the development of discourse and dialogue in the household, and in the coparticipation of family members in the life of the household that Swanson believes the very capacities and dispositions for constructive public participation are formed.

Swanson's thesis suggests a reconsideration of Arendt's, and perhaps Sennett's, views of the private. The present malaise of the public is due, in part, to a malaise of the private; the private realm is simply not in a sufficiently healthy condition to prompt and sustain an invigorated public. Assuming that this point has merit, one does not then go about the restoration of the public merely by reforming or revitalizing public practices and institutions; one must attend as well to the reinvigoration of private life. Hence the restoration of the public calls for a consideration of many things private, such as the nature of the household (for example, the character and quality of adult-child interactions that take place there), the possibility for and character of work (in the sense of employment and jobs), and the role and place of spiritual sustenance (particularly religion).

In contending that the restoration of a public requires consideration equal to that given the restoration of the private, I am maintaining a substantial distinction between these two entities. There are, however, those who find this division between public and private a troubling one, even with the refurbished image of the private suggested here. Their arguments raise the question of whether a strong difference between private and public life is really as important to the health of democracy as is believed by so many of the theorists previously cited. A sympathetic consideration of these alternative arguments provides a fascinating look at how deeply the issues surrounding public and private penetrate into the general conditions for human flourishing.

Let us begin to look at the contrary position by imagining a critic of the proposition that healthy private and public spheres are jointly necessary for a high quality of life in a democracy. Consider her contention that the values required to sustain healthy private and public spaces are the same, as are the mechanisms for acquiring these values. Given this sameness, there is no need to distinguish between public and private life. Indeed to do so benefits primarily men, as they have typically been the ones who occupy the public spaces. In occupying the public spaces, men gain and hold the authority to rule, and thereby come into possession of the means to limit membership in the public sphere. This limiting of membership frequently takes the form of excluding women, as well as other males who do not share the views, traits, or identifying marks of the men with power.

Continuing her rebuttal, our critic asserts distinct advantages for a single sphere. This sphere would be founded on one or a very few extremely important values to be held in common by all members of the sphere. Candidates for such values include caring, nurturance, respect, love, and regard. If these values characterized human beings and their relationships with one another, there would be little need to draw the public-private distinction, for public life would be a mere extrapolation of the good private life, and vice versa. As matters now stand, these values are more evident in the private sphere, while values such as fairness, justice, and equality are the evident values in the public sphere. This bifurcation is morally wrong, she argues, because it permits, perhaps even encourages, forms of domination and subjugation that no truly civil, properly democratic society should tolerate.

This criticism parallels the critique offered by several feminist writers, although these writers touch only occasionally on the distinction between public and private. Donna Kerr, for example, contends that "liberalism does not help us understand how to nurture our own lives, or the lives of others."[19] Kerr believes that nurturance ought to be the core concept for sustaining civility. In so arguing, she finds liberal conceptions of democracy wanting, and thereby casts considerable doubt on the need to separate the private from the public life.

In arguing for a reconstructed view of domestic tranquility, Jane Roland Martin develops a thesis that also rejects the split between public and private. Martin states that "social reality demands that we expand the founding fathers' understanding of domestic tranquility and that we reclaim the civic or public realm as a domestic domain."[20] In Martin's view, to the extent that school is conceived as a place that prepares the young for civic or public life, it "teaches them to devalue that place called home and the things associated with it."[21] She argues that it would be far better if the values and responsibilities of enlightened domestic life became the values of an enlightened civic life.

In her ground-breaking efforts to develop a feminine basis for ethics and moral education, Nel Noddings advances notions about caring[22] that bear on the public-private distinction in much the same way that Kerr's and Martin's do (although there are important differences among their respective philosophical positions). Noddings finds that the currently dominant political values of justice and fairness permit persons to engage in a range of inhumane acts toward one another. In place of these values, she would adopt the ethic of caring, a form of relational regard between and among persons that would prohibit the moral travesties that today's civic morality appears to allow. Although Noddings does not specifically address the public-private distinction, her argument clearly implies the inappropriateness of separating the two. The ethic of caring, properly applied, obviates the need for a difference between public and private.

The work of Kerr, Martin, and Noddings raises a fascinating set of questions, questions that must be tackled before we too blithely engage in the work of restoring public life in American society or of revitalizing the difference between public and private life. Among these questions is the one posed by Rodney King after the violence that erupted when a jury found innocent the police who were videotaped beating him with clubs: "Can't we all just get along?" he asked. A moment's reflection on this question suggests that we have a number of options for how we might all just get along.

For example, suppose that nurturance, domestic tranquility, or caring is sufficient for us all to "just get along." In this case, it seems unnecessary to pose a dual life: one private and largely domestic, the other public and largely civic. We can get along in the public sphere in the same way we get along in the private sphere, wherein what permits us to act in common with one another is a mutual desire to know, understand, care for, and sustain one another. On the other hand, suppose that the values argued for most strongly by feminist scholars are dependent on a sort of preexisting relational bond, such as family, love, or close friendship. In this case, we would need different values if we are to forge a relationship with those who are outside our circles of family, loved ones, and good friends. On what basis do we all just get along with those outside these circles?

One way to answer this question rather effectively is to posit a difference between private and public spheres, wherein a public sphere is created so that we can transact human affairs grounded in relationships outside the boundaries of family, loved ones, and close friends. Indeed, a public sphere of this kind may be required to realize many of the promises of democratic life, wherein we are often required to transact affairs with people with whom we disagree, are in competition, or differ on religious, racial, social, sexual, or other grounds. To transact these human affairs in ways most likely to allow each of us as individuals to pursue our own conceptions of the good life calls for a public realm of some kind, a place where we may meet and, while agreeing to disagree, employ common speech, common values, and common sense to maintain and nourish both neighborhood and nationhood.

There appear to be two views of human nature and human possibility here. One view, represented by several of the feminist scholars mentioned above, believes very strongly in the classic, ideal values of home and hearth, positing these values as foundational for all human relationships. On this view, there is no need for a difference between private and public life, and there is a grave possibility that the persistence of this distinction is harmful to the true ideals of democratic life. The other view holds that the values so intimately associated with hearth and home will not serve well to sustain the transaction of political, social, and economic affairs.[23] These values, it is argued, are dependent on certain forms of human relationship that do not obtain in the public sphere. Absent these relationships, the values will not work as a basis for regulating human interaction.

It is almost as if the protagonists, those who argue for a refurbished differentiation between private and public, are positioning themselves as hard-nosed empiricists, saying something like, "Sure, it would be wonderful if ideal domestic values could regulate human exchange in public settings, but it just does not work. And because it does not work, we need to build our public spaces on norms and values that will work there." The antagonists, those who argue against the public-private distinction by proposing a universality of ideal domestic values, rebut this claim with the contention that the antagonists settle too easily for the world as it is, rather than how it might be. They argue, "You say it will not work, but it could if we aspired to it, if we were willing to try. We agree that it does not work now, but we disagree that it cannot work. Consider what is gained by trying, for our position holds far more potential for ultimate human flourishing than what you say are the facts of the matter."

The issues posed by this dispute are important, powerful, and provocative. They demand that we ponder the public-private distinction with great care. At the same time, we are not free to sit by, watching the fabric of democratic life unravel while we deliberate on various possibilities for eliciting human goodness. Until the issues come into sharper focus, with some agreement on the grounds for resolving them, we must choose and act. For me the choice is to restore the differences between public and private, but not through some simplistic scheme to bring back family values or to revitalize the teaching of history and civics in our schools. These are important, but they are artifacts of a restoration, not the restoration itself. The restoration itself must take place in the private, domestic sphere as well as in the public sphere.

In the private sphere, the restoration must involve decent and dignified conceptions of parenting and child rearing; it must provide time and opportunity for children and adults to build bonds of love and understanding; it must take place in settings that are safe; and it must include some minimal freedom from want. In the public sphere, it must acknowledge the value of difference while seeking the basis for commonness; it must permit us to communicate with one another without inflicting physical harm or psychological trauma; and it must challenge us to see that our individual visions of the good life are interdependent with the health of our communities, our states, our nation, and our world.

The accomplishment of these ends requires a public education that is attentive to both the private and public spheres: an education that does not glorify one and impugn the other, but serves as a bridge between them. As a result of a good public education, one ought to be better prepared for both realms of life, for, as I have argued here, the success of both is requisite to the success of either. On this view, it matters not whether the education of the young is financed publicly or privately, by taxes or tuition, by warrants or by vouchers. The point is that *all* schools, no matter how financed or how governed, are public schools in the sense that they bear a responsibility for the creation of a public within American society.

It is vital to democratic governance that we distinguish between "in here" and "out there." The difference is essential to realizing the promises of a liberal democracy.[24] At the same time, we should be attentive to the possibility that a liberal democracy is not the form of democracy that ought to be continued in the United States. Nor should we necessarily continue the tight difference between private and public spheres that a liberal democracy seems to require. Thus while we are attending to the restoration of private and public realms, as a way of ameliorating the times in which we now live and that we anticipate for the near future, we must also be attentive to the possibilities for their eventual dissolution. This dissolution should come about as the result of a conception of human possibility and democratic governance superior to the ones that now regulate human transactions. Until that time is at hand, however, the better part of wisdom appears to be to restore what we have lost, in a way that does not carry the same troubling consequences as those suffered in an earlier time.

Notes

1. Joel Spring, *The American School, 1642–1993*, 3d ed. (New York: McGraw-Hill, 1994), p. 99.
2. Richard Sennett, *The Fall of Public Man* (New York: Knopf, 1977).
3. Meg Greenfield, "It's Time for Some Civility," *Newsweek*, 5 June 1995, p. 78.
4. H. Brandt Ayers, "The Death of Civility," *New York Times*, 16 July 1994, p. 14.
5. Molly Ivins, "New Incivility Shows Only More Cowardice," *Arizona Daily Star*, 17 April 1995, p. A-9.
6. Robert F. Durant, "The Democratic Deficit in America," *Political Science Quarterly* 110 (Spring 1995): 1, 25–47.

7. Benjamin R. Barber, *An Aristocracy of Everyone: The Politics of Education and the Future of America* (New York: Ballantine Books, 1992), p. 15.
8. Jean Bethke Elshtain, *Democracy on Trial* (New York: Basic Books, 1995), p. xii.
9. John Rawls, *Political Liberalism* (New York: Columbia University Press, 1993), p. xvi.
10. It is probably not necessary to point out that the use of the term *liberal* in this context does not mean what it means when it is used to draw a distinction with *conservative*. When modifying "democracy," the term liberal points to that form of democracy that stresses the welfare of the individual over that of the group or community. See Stephen Mulhall and Adam Swift, *Liberals and Communitarians* (Cambridge, Mass.: Blackwell, 1992).
11. Robert Westbrook, "Public Schooling and American Democracy," in *Democracy, Education, and the Schools*, ed. Roger Soder (San Francisco: Jossey-Bass, 1996), p. 125.
12. Walter Feinberg, "The Moral Responsibility of Public Schools," in *The Moral Dimensions of Teaching*, eds. John I. Goodlad, Roger Soder, and Kenneth A. Sirotnik (San Francisco: Jossey-Bass, 1990), p. 181.
13. For a further elaboration on the loss of connection between democracy and schooling, see Gary D Fenstermacher, *The Absence of Democratic and Educational Ideals from Contemporary Educational Reform Initiatives*, the 1994 Stanley Elam Lecture (Glassboro, N.J.: EdPress, 1994); reprinted in *Record in Educational Leadership* 15 (Spring/Summer 1995): 26–34. See also various chapters in Soder, ed., *Democracy, Education, and the Schools*.
14. Westbrook, "Public Schooling and American Democracy," p. 125.
15. David C. Berliner and Bruce J. Biddle, *The Manufactured Crisis: Myths, Fraud, and the Attack on America's Public Schools* (Reading, Mass.: Addison-Wesley, 1995), p. xii.
16. Hannah Arendt, *The Human Condition* (Chicago: University of Chicago Press, 1958).

17. It is no easy matter to sort out Arendt's views on the relative standing of the private and public realms of human life. She certainly recognizes the intimate connection between the two and acknowledges that critical life activities take place in the private realm. As best as I am able to ascertain, however, she does not see the private realm as a place where the young are prepared for participation in the public realm. The larger issue here is not whether the private is simply a logical necessity for there to be a public, but whether a private realm of a certain kind is required to have a public realm of a certain kind; that is, whether a particular kind of private life is required for the formation of a public of the kind Arendt so obviously reveres.
18. Judith A. Swanson, *The Public and the Private in Aristotle's Political Philosophy* (Ithaca, N.Y.: Cornell University Press, 1992).
19. Donna Kerr, "Democracy, Nurturance, and Community," in Soder, ed., *Democracy, Education, and the Schools*, p. 39.
20. Jane Roland Martin, "Education for Domestic Tranquility," in *Critical Conversations in Philosophy of Education*, ed. Wendy Kohli (New York: Routledge, 1995), p. 49.
21. Martin, "Education for Domestic Tranquility," p. 53.
22. See Nel Noddings, *Caring* (Berkeley: University of California Press, 1984); and *The Challenge to Care in Schools* (New York: Teachers College Press, 1992).
23. It is tempting to point out that this other view is held primarily by males, though it would be an error to do so. Jean Bethke Elshtain and Judith Swanson are among the advocates for a distinction between public and private realms. The difference between the two views is not grounded in the sex of the scholars, but in the place they give to gender as a lens for studying and resolving this issue.
24. For a compelling and highly illuminating argument on this point, see Theodore J. Lowi, *The End of the Republican Era* (Norman: University of Oklahoma Press, 1995).

Chapter Five

Toward a Democratic Rhetoric of Schooling

Donna H. Kerr

John Stuart Mill was concerned about "the unspeakable ignorance and inattention of [humankind] in respect to the influences which form human character."[1] In this chapter, I express a similar concern. We tend to talk about democracy as a political hope and about how to school ourselves to support democracy. In using such rhetoric, we predispose schooling both to fail our political hopes and to fail as an educational institution. We need, I will argue, a new rhetoric of schooling, one that shuns the fantasy of using political ideals to form and correct human beings and attends instead to the social and psychological realities that ground the development of self, soul, and character. Further, it is only by attending to these realities of the psyche that schools can truly educate and democracy becomes possible.

Between You and Me

Recently, in boarding a late-night shuttle from San Francisco to Seattle, I found myself in line behind a woman in her mid-twenties. Her exceedingly short hair, glowing a neon carrot color, seemed in character with her ear and nose studs. My hair is reasonably short and its chestnut color natural, with an occasional post-fifty white hair that I almost always remove on discovery. She

I wish to acknowledge that through several conversations and criticisms of a draft, Margret Buchmann contributed substantially to the evolution of this chapter.

wore a skimpy black halter, black tights, a short black studded leather jacket, and black combat boots. I, in contrast, was dressed casually but properly: a skirt and sweater; comfortable but feminine shoes; a long Ono Mik scarf (being tall, I feel elegant in long scarves); and a Chinese necklace to complement the beautiful Asian design of my silken scarf.

Ours being the last zone to board the airplane, the line stood still long enough for me to catch myself in the process of casting this young woman as foreign, unrelated to me. Uncomfortable in what I thereby perceived in myself, I looked again. Her skin, scrubbed and freckled, could have been that of a youngster riding the bus to school with my nine-year-old daughter. Likely aware of my gaze, she turned around and our eyes met. Hers were a light clear blue—the blue of my grandmother's eyes—eyes that as a child I wished that I had inherited as had my older sister. Did this young person cast me out as an unrelated "other," as I nearly had her?

So who is an "other"? To begin, it is someone who is not me. If you are not me, who are you? If you are not me, must I fear you? Hide from you? Control you? Or, possibly, fix you? If I must fear you, then I must keep track of you by clearly marking you as something other than myself. The sources of my fear or discomfort, whatever they are, make me want to distance me from you. In *Outcasts: Signs of Otherness in Northern European Art of the Late Middle Ages*, Ruth Mellinkoff observes the depiction of secular fools in outlandishly unfashionable clothing, for example, in the parti-colored, striped costumes similar to jesters' garb in decks of playing cards.[2] These secular fools served as entertainers and moral critics, whose satires and parodies of lives in their society made audiences uncomfortable. By casting such a critic as the strange other, one might then disconnect, cease to be too uncomfortable about what the other might reflect about oneself or one's society. Do the meanings that I assigned to the clothing and accoutrements of the young woman whom I observed as I boarded the shuttle protect me from the true sources of my discomfort, from myself? Do I delude myself in casting her as foreign to me, so as not to face a part of myself? Do I project my "evil" onto her? Might I go so far as to think that it would be better for us all if she might be corrected (schooled?) to be more like . . . well, me—or me as I like to think of myself? Might not I even describe my efforts as a form of caring? Failing her rehabilitation, in frustration, might I go so far as to blame her for things that bother me, much as Henry Ford blamed the Jews for most everything that bothered Henry Ford? Such currents in a morally troubled psyche cannot support democratic relations among persons.

A Proposal in the Face of Confounding Rhetoric

I propose that how we think about you and me and how we regard one another determines whether democracy is a real possibility or just another in a string of political myths. However, from listening to the prevailing rhetoric about schooling and democracy, one would never understand democracy as something that speaks to human relationships and the related structure of the psyche. Consider, for example, several salient ways of thinking about the connection between schooling and democracy.

One such approach to linking education and democracy calls on the schools to prepare students to participate in a democracy. Generally, that preparation is taken to include such things as knowledge of how the institutions of democracy work, a belief in the importance of participating by developing informed opinions and exercising one's right to vote, a disposition to abide by laws that protect us from one another, and familiarity with the history and basic documents of the particular democracy in which the students live. (In the United States, these documents would include, among others, the Constitution and the Bill of Rights.) In some contexts, these lists of knowledge, skills, and dispositions include even the appreciation of capitalism as the economic form underlying democracy. This approach assumes that if we know how to run democracy's machinery and how to inform ourselves, and if we are inclined to be law-abiding, an actual democracy will follow. To the contrary, I suggest that a person can fact-find, vote, and obey the law, yet still live a life constituted not by democratic relationships, but rather by those of domination and subservience.

A second way to connect democracy and education calls for the schooling of all individuals so that each can make a contribution to society. Supplying all persons with knowledge and skills to participate in society is argued to be both fair and necessary to the functioning of a democracy. The democratic impulse is clear in this line of reasoning. It is less clear how simply equipping all people with some kinds of knowledge and skills might translate into a democracy, particularly one where contributions would be valued in ways reflecting democratic relations among those involved. We can treat others as inferior by the ways in which we receive their contributions. It is unclear, furthermore, how socially valuable knowledge might guard against the labeling, hence the treatment, of some persons in prejudicial ways. The connections among socially valuable learnings and the relational qualities of a democracy seem tenuous and indirect.

Another view defines schooling as an important tool for protecting the nation supposedly at risk because of fierce economic competition, foreign military might, and internal threats. The idea here is that by protecting the nation we protect democracy and, to complete the circle, that we can protect democracy by developing the kinds of knowledge and skills that will protect the nation's status in the world. Under this view, a democracy needs to be populated with persons of considerable instrumental knowledge so that "our team" can and will win. Here we see more concern for protecting the nation than for promoting democracy itself, more concern for schooling's role as the handmaiden of a dominant nation than for its possible educative powers in the building of a democracy. Many strong, avowedly democratic nations have not only condoned relations of domination and subservience but have also fostered them through institutions and policies.

Finally, a significantly different proposal for how education and democracy might be linked is just beginning to find its way into the rhetoric of schooling. It seems to respond to recent work in political theory, for example, Robert Putnam's *Making Democracy Work* and, likely soon to join the references, Francis Fukuyama's *Trust*.[3] These works identify certain features of civil society that affect a society's prospects for democracy or prosperity. Putnam studied regional governments in Italy from 1970 to 1990. In trying to account for why they seem to work well in the north but not in the south of Italy, he comes to the conclusion that a more robustly civil society, as evidenced by higher levels of participation in voluntary associations for hundreds of years, accounts for the difference. With this view of what makes democracy work, what, then, might be said of the connection between schooling and democracy? Rather than being misled by single-factor accounting, we should start with the notion that the robustness of civility is at least one major factor. Schools ought, then, to be breeding grounds for civility.

There is a morally interesting shift in rhetoric when schools are thought to promote civility as a way to underwrite democracy, for civility rings of human relations apparently more obviously than, in the salient rhetoric, does democracy. Attending to the mediating role of civility helps us to avoid the error of leaping over or ignoring human needs and focusing directly and exclusively on the requirements of operating political and economic institutions. Hence, the rhetoric of civility is morally significant. However, there are also disturbing features in this way of thinking about schooling. It suggests that by encouraging the stuff of civil society that, for example, Putnam identifies, we will be supporting democracy. Sadly, not all civil societies are democratic in nature. As Fareed Zakaria notes in response to Putnam in his review of Fukuyama's *Trust*, "The Italian north has been better run than the Italian south for hundreds of years, during which time the country was, to put it mildly, not always democratic."[4] That is, from the fact that a school might function as a strong community, it does not follow that such a community will support, much less encourage, democracy in human relationships. Not uncommonly, communities are held together by a measure of domination that renders them morally suspect.

Rhetoric that considers schooling instrumental to civil society—which, in turn, is instrumental to democracy—misses a fundamental moral point. If persons live in relationships of domination and subservience, no rhetoric of democracy can render their relations democratic. Thus, even hopeful talk of schooling for civility disregards the moral character of democracy, namely that democracy pertains to how we human beings *are* with and toward one another. To exemplify this point, let us return to me and the young woman in line to take the shuttle to Seattle. I might belong to a host of voluntary associations and still fail to stand in a democratic relationship—one of mutuality—with this young woman. In our voluntary associations we may be racist, sexist bigots who cast certain others as inferior or in need of correction; that we engage with others is no guarantee that such exchanges will have a benign character. Indeed, we might choose to associate only with those who seem most like us in our antidemocratic leanings. Hence, we are still left with the question of how to think of and talk about the relationship between education and democracy, between the formation of human beings and the prospect for lives of mutual regard.

The Moral Meanings of Education and Democracy

The moral grounds for institutional and other political arrangements of a democracy, for all their historical complexity, can be stated succinctly in both the negative and the positive. The negative rendering is this: one should neither dominate nor be subservient to another, neither use another nor be used by another. Stated in the positive (though not in any sense equivalent) form: persons have a right to relationships of mutuality. The latter is underwritten by the psychological fact that for the self to develop, the soul to flourish, and character to evolve (mostly overlapping, highly interconnected matters), a person needs a social context of psychological democracy—that is, a person needs to stand in at least some relationships of mutual regard. This means that to develop as persons, humans need at least some relationships that are free of domination.

The development and flourishing of the self, the soul, and character—necessary features of moral life, including democratic relationships—depend upon one's experiencing relationships of mutuality, upon what some would choose to call generosity, trust, and respect, and yet others (in whose numbers am I) would boldly term love. Yes, short of love—love free from domination—democracy is a failed project. We need, therefore, to be concerned centrally with the conditions that foster the development of the self and the education of the soul or character. Here I am saying two things, one that makes a point about education and the other about democracy. Martin Buber argues the first: "Education worthy of the name is essentially education of character."[5] The second is that hopes for democracy depend upon our giving up domination and subservience in favor of mutuality, a point that Jessica Benjamin argues richly in *Bonds of Love*.[6] I turn now to Buber and Benjamin to offer a sense of what a moral rhetoric of education and democracy would bring into public discourse. Here I cannot present the full argument, but I want to suggest the issues with which such a moral rhetoric would face us.

Let us imagine that Buber is right, that the only education worthy of its name is the education of character. To appreciate the idea, we do not have to discard the notion that there might be considerable value in the sorts of learnings that are celebrated on achievement tests and in talk of multiple intelligences and the like. That is simply not where a moral rhetoric would focus. A person highly schooled in the standard curriculum would not necessarily be what Buber calls a "great character," that is, "one who by his actions and attitudes satisfies the claim of situations out of deep readiness to respond with his whole life, and in such a way that the sum of his actions and attitudes expresses at the same time the unity of his being in its willingness to accept responsibility."[7] Being whole persons, great characters (and great teachers) are not subservient to others—a state of abdication of self-responsibility that renders the soul sterile. ("And," as Buber notes, "a sterile soul soon ceases to be a soul."[8]) Nor do they dominate others, but are responsive to them. The various forms of political domination (such as totalitarianism) deny persons both unity of the self and responsibility, but "great and full" relations between human beings can exist only between whole, responsible persons. Hence, "genuine education of character is genuine education for community," but not just any sort of community.[9] It must be a community of persons who neither feel a need to control others nor require the direction of others to feel whole. It is, I submit, genuine education for a community made up of *democratic relationships*.

With such a moral rhetoric of education, new questions would arise. The education of character, not being the stuff of lesson plans and course syllabi, would require a different sort of talk about teaching. As Buber suggests, "For educating characters you do not need [to be] a moral genius, but you do need [to be] a man who is wholly alive and able to communicate himself directly to his fellow beings."[10] Further, educating character "demands presence, responsibility; it demands you."[11] In this moral rhetoric of education, then, talk would turn to such questions as these: What is it to be wholly alive? How are we to understand what it means to be truly present to and for another human being? (Might that itself be an expression of love?) What does it mean to be responsible for oneself and responsive to others? Preparation to be a teacher would be thought, for example, to consist importantly in struggling to become whole oneself and in the related capacity to be present to others. It would be no less than an education of the soul, or character. That is, whether one could educate others would depend upon how one is with oneself and others. Deeper human issues would pervade the rhetoric of educating.

What if one appreciates the power of Buber's understanding of the education of character and still thinks of the link between schooling and democracy as being adequately encompassed by the standard rhetoric? I would argue that such a stance miscasts the nature of domination and tears the moral core out of democracy. As Benjamin points out, Freud gave us a basis for comprehending that domination is a product not of human nature, but of human relationships.[12] If we agree with Buber that a person's character is shaped in community—in human relationships—and if we understand that democracy, as opposed to domination and subservience, is similarly a manner and mode of human relationships, we begin to see the moral connection between education and democracy. Democracy is possible only through the formation of character, democratic character. Such formation takes place in interactions of a certain sort between persons. It is *not* born of knowing how to run the machinery of democracy, of standing prepared to make contributions, of being loaded with powerful instrumental knowledge, or of voluntarily associating with others.

Democracy makes demands of you and me. Drawing from Benjamin, we can think of prospects for democracy turning on how you and I deal with our simultaneous need for recognition and independence. It involves, to use Benjamin's words, "the most fateful paradox" that you are outside my control and yet I need you to recognize me, inasmuch as individuals grow in and through their relationships with others. In dominating, I resolve the paradox by trying to control you, so that I can get the recognition I want. Alternatively, if I am the dominated, I resolve the paradox by letting you control me so that I can gain your recognition. The democratic resolution makes our ties "not shackles, but circuits of recognition."[13] That is, we engage in mutual recognition or, when we fail at that, we at least stand willing to address the difficulties of recognizing one another. Put otherwise, the democratic psyche, formed in human relationships, is both receptive of the other and self-expressive. Genuine hope for democracy is grounded in this circuit of recognition. To jump over this reality in favor of talk of civil society and the requirements of political life is to fail to acknowledge the psychic and social realities in which democratic relations take root, when they do. That is, political actions, such as enacting civil rights legislation, can outlaw certain forms of domination but cannot themselves generate the conditions that nourish the mutuality in human relations that, in turn, constitutes the moral backbone of democracy.

Concluding Note

The so-called democracy superimposed upon human relationships of the dominating and dominated is democratic in form only, not in content. If democracy is to have substance, it can come only through the development of relations of mutual recognition and regard. To the extent that schools are staffed by adults who have the moral capacity to be wholly alive and to be present to young persons (most likely and commonly one at a time), the schools can be places where persons can grow in character and soul and where a democracy of substance can take root. Interestingly, public institutions other than schools may be more hospitable to the education of character. I have in mind, for example, some loosely organized church groups where adults basically hang out with children, neighborhood youth organizations such as those described by Milbrey McLaughlin and colleagues in *Urban Sanctuaries*,[14] and some community centers. Such places are concerned simply with availing children of self-responsible, responsive adults—unlike schools, which too commonly shackle adults and children with habits of control, rationalized programs, and detailed planning. Curiously, schools as we generally know them may have little to do with the education of the soul or character and, hence, little to do with the substantive development of democracy. What a very odd thing to have to say about public schools, whose justification lies in our wanting to create or maintain a democracy.

Notes

1. John Stuart Mill, *The Subjection of Women* (London, 1869), pp. 39–40, as quoted in Richard Wollheim, *The Mind and Its Depths* (Cambridge, Mass.: Harvard University Press, 1993), p. 194.

2. Ruth Mellinkoff, *Outcasts: Signs of Otherness in Northern European Art of the Late Middle Ages*, vol. 1: *Text* (Berkeley: University of California Press, 1993), esp. pp. 28–31.
3. Robert D. Putnam with Robert Leonardi and Raffaella Y. Nanetti, *Making Democracy Work: Civic Traditions in Modern Italy* (Princeton: Princeton University Press, 1993); and Francis Fukuyama, *Trust: The Social Virtues and the Creation of Prosperity* (New York: Free Press, 1995).
4. Fareed Zakaria, "Bigger Than the Family, Smaller Than the State," *New York Times Book Review*, 13 August 1995, p. 25.
5. Martin Buber, "The Education of Character" in *Between Man and Man* (New York: Macmillan, 1965), p. 104.
6. Jessica Benjamin, *Bonds of Love: Psychoanalysis, Feminism, and the Problem of Domination* (New York: Pantheon Books, 1988).
7. Buber, "The Education of Character," p. 114.
8. Buber, "The Education of Character," p. 115.
9. Buber, "The Education of Character," p. 116.
10. Buber, "The Education of Character," p. 105.
11. Buber, "The Education of Character," p. 114.
12. Benjamin, *Bonds of Love*, p. 5.
13. Benjamin, *Bonds of Love*, p. 221.
14. Milbrey W. McLaughlin, Merita A. Irby, and Juliet Langman, *Urban Sanctuaries: Neighborhood Organizations in the Lives and Futures of Inner-City Youth* (San Francisco: Jossey-Bass, 1994).

Chapter Six

Democracy

Do We Really Want It?

Roger Soder

I advance here three claims. First, we are not born with a working knowledge of our rights and duties as citizens in a democracy; these are matters that must be learned if a people is to be able to govern itself wisely. Second, the place where these matters are most effectively learned is schools. Third, if schools are the primary locus of learning, then we must determine what teachers need to know to prepare students for citizenship in a democracy. These three claims, familiar to us all, are nonetheless conclusory. They are conclusory in themselves, and they are conclusory in that they assume the capability and the desirability of a people to govern itself. It is this fundamental assumption, above all, that needs attention. I submit that there are many among academicians, politicians, and policymakers who will, in the end, argue that the assumption is fundamentally incorrect. It is thus that I derive the question in the title of this chapter, do we really want democracy in America?

We must in the first place talk about the nature of a people and its capabilities for political constitution. The question, Hamilton tells us in the first of the Federalist papers, is whether a people can establish good government on the basis of reflection and choice or must forever depend on accident and force.

The question centers on the capacity of a people to govern itself well. The "well" here is of great importance. (As it is with Hamilton: he talks not of government but of *good* government.) A people can govern itself, but what of that? If the concept of quality is not an integral part of self-governance, then not much will have been gained. If people are not kept secure from random violence, what then of self-governance? An angry and armed mob or a band of thieves can be self-governing. If the poor and infirm are not attended to, what then? If cholera is widespread because people would rather spend money on self-amusement than on securing a safe supply of water and the safe disposal of wastes, what then of self-governance?

What can we say of a people that governs itself well? First, to be self-governing is to be free. There are, of course, various meanings of the word freedom. For our purposes, it can be defined, as Herbert Muller has construed it in *The Issues of Freedom*, as "the condition of being able to choose and carry out purposes."[1] This in turn involves the absence of external constraints, actual ability combined with actual means, and conscious choice. There are, then, two requirements to be free. People must have the power to exercise freedom. And people must have the insight to value freedom. Without power, one can value freedom but do little about one's situation. If freedom is not valued and is not seen as worth fighting for, one will not seek to minimize external constraints, one will not seek ability and means, one will not make conscious choices.

Second, a people must know its rights and the implications of those rights. As Ralph Lerner and Philip Kurland point out in *The Founders' Constitution*, a language of rights "presupposes a particular kind of speaker and audience. Claimants must be mindful of what is due them; governors must be reminded that they govern a people who know what is due them."[2]

Third, a people that governs itself well knows the difference between a persuaded audience and a more thoughtful public. Is the audience in Rome after Mark Antony's speech in *Julius Caesar* a more thoughtful public? How about the mob that goes after Colonel Sherburn in *Huckleberry Finn?* What might we say about the crowds at the Nazi rallies at Nuremberg in the 1930s? A more thoughtful public might well be a persuaded public, but it is a public acting on reason, a public allowing itself consciously to be persuaded, knowing the implications of what it is being asked to give its assent.

A more thoughtful public knows how to demand more of itself—and knows how to demand more of its leaders. What is due a more thoughtful public is not only its rights but, in a larger sense, more thoughtful leadership.

These notions about freedom and rights and self-governance and a thoughtful public involve conclusory claims. The claims have been—and continue to be—contested. For every claim for freedom and a more thoughtful public there are voices offering opposition. And of these voices, the most powerful for me is that of Dostoevsky's Grand Inquisitor. In one of the most compelling monologues in all of literature, Ivan Karamazov tells us of the return of Christ to Spain during the time of the Inquisition. The people flock to him in welcome. The Grand Inquisitor has Christ arrested and, in the middle of the night, he comes to the dungeon. Why have you come back, the Inquisitor asks. We have done what you failed to do. When you refused the temptations in the desert, you in effect offered the people choice, you offered them freedom. We know better and we have corrected your error. The people do not want the burden of freedom; the people want security and happiness. The people want to be ruled, not by themselves, but by us, in the name of miracle, mystery, and authority. The Grand Inquisitor concludes by telling Christ to go away and never come back.

In our own time, we have versions of the Grand Inquisitor's views. We have, for example, Singapore. In Singapore, there are rules, regulations, punishments. A place for everyone and everyone in his or her place. Better to have security and a limited kind of happiness—and limited freedom. In Singapore, a reporter for the *International Herald Tribune* is fined for writing a story suggesting that there are some corrupt judges in the Far East. Not only is the reporter fined, but the owners of the *Tribune*—the *New York Times* and the *Washington Post*—also submit a groveling apology to Singapore's leaders. Why bother with freedom of the press as long as the streets are safe (and as long as you can sell your now-safe newspapers)? There is no gainsaying the economic advances that have been made in Singapore, any more than there are most certainly reasonable arguments to be made against muggings in Central Park. On the other hand, we need to be careful lest we find ourselves comfortable with building autobahns and making the trains run on time.

Tocqueville (of course) warned us about such matters in *Democracy in America:* unless we were careful, he said, we would end up being "no more than a flock of timid and hardworking animals."[3] Tocqueville also warned us that despite the apparent acceptance of the claims for democracy and equality, there are those among the aristocracy who are only hiding, as would be immediately apparent were democracy to fall: "For all this conventional enthusiasm and obsequious formality toward the dominant power, it is easy to see that the rich have a great distaste for their country's democratic institutions. The people are a power whom they fear and scorn."[4]

I emphasize these counterclaims not as an obligatory obeisance to the other side, but because the counterclaims have, I believe, an acceptance wider than we might want to think. Despite all the talk about democracy and the American Way of Life and fighting for freedom, there are strong sentiments in favor of elitism and in support of the notion that the people simply cannot know. These sentiments are captured quite nicely in Kazuo Ishiguro's *The Remains of the Day:* we are told that it is not that the butler's opinion is right or wrong but that he simply *cannot* have an opinion (a notion with which, apparently, the butler agrees).[5] Others have expressed concern about the emergence and spread of elitism. Thus, in *An Aristocracy of Everyone*, Benjamin Barber argues that Allan Bloom and all the other followers of Leo Strauss feel very strongly (although very carefully) that most people cannot learn or at least cannot learn very much. The position Barber attributes to Bloom and the Straussians is: "To the educable, an education; to the rest, protection from fearsome truths through inoculation by half-truths."[6] Barber, of course, joins here a long line of critics of Bloom and elitism.

My concern, however, is that an unwillingness to accept that the people can indeed know and judge and engage in intelligent self-governance is hardly limited to the usual suspects among the Straussians. I am more inclined to think that there are a good many academicians, politicians, foundation people, and power brokers throughout the country who do not have, at heart, very much faith at all in the notion that "the people shall judge." There are many who would agree with Edmund Burke's assessment of the capacity of the people: in *Reflections on the Revolution in France*, Burke speaks of the people as "thousands of great cattle, reposed beneath the shadow of the British oak, [who] chew the cud, and are silent."[7] And many would agree with Lonesome Rhodes, the charismatic folksinger, con artist, and politician in Budd Schulberg's prescient 1957 movie, *A Face in the Crowd:* "I could throw them dog food and make them think they were eating steak." Lonesome isn't alone, as is reflected some years later by Richard Nixon in his musings about the people as children needing to be led by a strong father, and as will be seen by even a casual reading of the professional spinmeister's journal, *Campaigns and Elections*.

Perhaps it will be argued that I am unnecessarily exercised over this matter of what people really believe. But if we choose to come down on the side of freedom and democracy and a more thoughtful public, then we need to talk about what these notions imply for desired civic behavior and attitudes of citizens, and we have to ask whether these are behaviors and attitudes that can and should be taught, or whether we know of these matters by birth. And it will be difficult to talk about what these notions imply if we first are not really quite clear about whether we (and others) in point of fact do believe in what we are saying.

Assuming that we do reject the Grand Inquisitor and those of today who speak in his name, then we are talking about the creation of a public that knows the worth of itself and its institutions. We are talking about a public that recognizes the need for political process, a public that understands allocation of scarce resources and the dangers of zero-sum games. In *The Thinking Revolutionary*,

Ralph Lerner talks of the "institutions, procedures, and habits of mind that go to make a political regime actual."[8] All three of these factors, and especially the third, are of great importance. Where are they to be learned? An aged and ageless text at the University of Chicago, *The People Shall Judge*,[9] argues it this way: If we are to have a democracy, people must be free. In order to be free, people have to be their own judges. If they are to judge well, they must be wise. Now, people are born free; they are not born wise. That is to say, then, people have freedom as an inherent natural right; it is not a positivist right determined and bestowed by others. But they are not born wise. There is little to suggest that we are born knowing our rights and duties as citizens in a democracy. These are matters that must be learned if a people is to be able to govern itself wisely.

Where are these matters to be learned? One response is to argue that they are to be learned by means of direct, if minor, participation in the process. Thus Richard Croker, the third boss of Tammany Hall, argued with a British newspaper editor in 1897:

> Think what New York is and what the people of New York are. One half, more than one half, are of foreign birth. We have thousands upon thousands of men who are alien born, who have no ties connecting them with the city or the State. They do not speak our language, they do not know our laws, [but] they are the raw material with which we have to build up the State. . . .
>
> There is no denying the service which Tammany has rendered to the Republic. There is no such organization for taking hold of the untrained friendless man and converting him into a citizen. Who else would do it if we did not? Think of the hundreds of thousands of foreigners dumped into our city. They are too old to go to school. There is not a mugwump in the city who would shake hands with them. They are alone, ignorant strangers, a prey to all manner of anarchical and wild notions.
>
> And Tammany looks after them for the sake of their vote, grafts them upon the Republic, makes citizens of them in short; and although you may not like our motives or our methods, what other

> agency is there by which so long a row could have been hoed so quickly or so well? If we go down into the gutter it is because there are men in the gutter, and you have got to go down where they are if you are to do anything with them.[10]

This way of teaching citizenship might have been effective—Croker certainly thought it was—and others in similar circumstances (for example, Mayor Richard J. Daley in Chicago in the 1960s) might have thought the arrangement sound. But this way of teaching is not satisfactory, not if we are looking for something more than keeping the lid on. Croker might have agreed with the views of Burke noted above, and he probably would have wondered what Tocqueville was worried about. But if we are looking for an active, engaged, knowing people, a people that knows its rights, then we must be bothered about the Croker approach. The approach is similar to that of the padrone system in southern Italy, as described in Robert Putnam's *Making Democracy Work*.[11] If you need something, you go to the padrone. Or, similarly, in a scene early on in *The Godfather, Part II*, we see the young Don Corleone buying fruit from a street peddler. The peddler gives him the fruit, refusing to take payment. Don Corleone expresses his thanks, and tells the peddler, "You need something, you come to me, we'll talk." There is *exchange* here, one of the factors Putnam and Marcel Mauss[12] and others have identified as critical to civic community, but it is a kind of exchange that does not lead to creating and sustaining an active and knowing people.

So we have to answer not only the Grand Inquisitor, but Croker. Croker asks, "Who else would do it if we did not?" He thinks that the untrained and the friendless are too old to go to school. But surely the young can be taught in school about the moral and intellectual responsibilities of living and working in a democracy. Educators can very well ask "Who else would do it if we did not?"

If it is the school's responsibility to teach matters of citizenship, then how are they to do this? What should happen in the school? This, of course, leads to another question: what should teachers have as part of their working knowledge, their repertoire, if they are to ensure that all children learn the moral and intellectual responsibilities of citizenship in a democracy?

I have tried to look at responses to these questions, not only in our own time, but back to the founding of the American republic. Surely our discussion is not the first to touch on questions of the relationship of the school and American democracy. What is curious to me is that the responses tend to be of the kind Abraham Lincoln gave in 1832 in his very first political address. Lincoln assured the good people of Sangamo County that "Upon the subject of education, not presuming to dictate any plan or system respecting it, I can only say that I view it as the most important subject which we as a people can be engaged in."[13] There must have been at least a few people in the audience who were wanting Lincoln to elaborate a bit. Lincoln, like those before and after him, was unwilling to go very far beyond the general nostrums—something to bear in mind given his very careful use of words.

What one finds is a general unwillingness to get very specific about what it is we want to have happen in schools. There is an even greater unwillingness to prescribe what we want teachers to have as a part of their working knowledge of matters civic and political.[14]

A common response is to say that, yes, these matters are important and we deal with them by trying to ensure that we have democratically run classrooms and schools. The emphasis in these responses tends to be on teaching in a democracy, with implications for grouping, tracking, and access to materials and programs. In other instances, the emphasis is on cooperative learning among students. One hears, too, responses focusing on cooperative work among staff and the rejection of authoritarian, top-down, hegemonic relationships (what Richard Weaver, in *The Ethics of Rhetoric*, refers to as "that uneasiness we feel in the presence of power").[15]

Now, there is nothing particularly wrong with wanting to have a democratically run classroom, one in which the voices of students are heard and respected. Surely we can agree that if we want children to learn their rights and responsibilities as citizens in a democracy, it makes little sense to place them in authoritarian, fascist, top-down environments. However, we must ask whether having a democratically run classroom or school will alone do the job. There are those who claim that they are preparing students for civic responsibility by having them vote on where to go on a field trip. It might well be that voting on the field trip leads to voting in an election. But surely there is much more to being a good citizen in a democracy than simply voting. If we come back again to Ralph Lerner and notions of "institutions, procedures, and habits of mind," then we see that citizens must have a good deal more than a propensity to vote.

As stated earlier, citizens in a democracy must have a strong sense of their rights and what they should expect from their leaders. They must have a strong sense of the fundamental notions of the democratic political process, including notions of equality, fairness, and due process, and, in the United States, separation of powers and an independent judiciary. And they must believe that they themselves are, with appropriate preparation, fully capable of governing themselves well.

There have been many approaches to outlining some of what both students and teachers specifically need to learn.[16] But the task, the worrisome task, is not simply the preparation of a curriculum for students and for those who intend to be teachers to ensure that all understand the fundamental moral and intellectual dimensions of citizenship in a democracy. Were that all that had to be done, it would have already been done. The difficulty, rather, is in the translation from curriculum outline to practice. We might say, with justification, that citizens in the American democracy need to have some basic knowledge of the Constitution of the United States, and thus it seems reasonable to insist that those who intend to teach need to have some knowledge of the Constitution as well as some sense of how they are going to address the matter in the schools. But, echoing the Watergate refrain, what should intending teachers know and when should they know it? What might count as acceptable levels of working knowledge of the Constitution? It is not unusual for a person now coming into a teacher education program to be thirty years old with an undergraduate degree from another institution earned some years earlier—someone whose formal civic education likely ended with American Government 100. How are we to assess this person's potential for teaching students civic competence?

These are difficulties that we need to address directly if we do indeed believe that teachers have a primary responsibility for preparing students for citizenship in a democracy. We have not addressed these difficulties. We have, as I have suggested, all too often preferred to substitute talk about democratic classrooms, cooperative work relationships, and a reduction of top-down authority for a serious confrontation with what it means to prepare teachers (and students) for civic responsibility.

There is perhaps a further, even less edifying, reason for a general reluctance to address these matters head on, a reason contained in the title of this chapter. Many people really do not believe in the worth of democracy in the first place. As a result, the problems are much like those faced, say, with trying to address the learning situation of African American children. There are those who put forth all sorts of approaches to curriculum and learning styles and multiculturalism, but who ignore the pervasive presence of those racist teachers who do not believe that African American children can learn. Is the problem simply finding better curricula or learning styles? Is the problem making sure that intending teachers have a course in multiculturalism? Or, rather, is not the problem that someone can mouth mantras such as "all children can learn" while believing, at heart, that some children inherently cannot learn very much at all? I am suggesting that just as there are people who do not believe in some children's ability to learn, there are those who do not believe that the people can rule and judge well for themselves. Therefore, comforting as it may be for some of us to develop required lists of texts that should be interrogated in general education and teacher education programs, we first have to understand that the problem is not simply determining what students and teachers should know. The problem is that among many academicians, politicians, and policymakers, there is a general belief that in some benign form, the Grand Inquisitor basically has it right.

Notes

1. Herbert Muller, *Issues of Freedom: Paradoxes and Promises* (New York: Harper & Brothers, 1960), p. 5.
2. Philip B. Kurland and Ralph Lerner, eds., *The Founders' Constitution*, vol. 1: *Major Themes* (Chicago: University of Chicago Press, 1987), p. 424.
3. Alexis de Tocqueville, *Democracy in America*, trans. George Lawrence (1835, 1840; reprint, New York: Anchor, 1969), p. 692.
4. Tocqueville, *Democracy in America*, p. 179.
5. Kazuo Ishiguro, *The Remains of the Day* (New York: Vintage Books, 1990).
6. Benjamin R. Barber, *An Aristocracy of Everyone: The Politics of Education and the Future of America* (New York: Ballantine Books, 1992), p. 174.
7. Edmund Burke, *Reflections on the Revolution in France*, ed. Thomas Mahoney (Indianapolis: Bobbs-Merrill, 1955), p. 97.
8. Ralph Lerner, *The Thinking Revolutionary: Principle and Practice in the New Republic* (Ithaca, N.Y.: Cornell University Press, 1987), p. 61.
9. Staff, Social Sciences 1, College of the University of Chicago, ed., *The People Shall Judge: Readings in the Formation of American Policy*, 2 vols. (Chicago: University of Chicago Press, 1949).
10. M. R. Werner, *Tammany Hall* (Garden City, N.Y.: Doubleday, Doran & Co., 1928), pp. 449–50.
11. Robert D. Putnam with Robert Leonardi and Raffaella Y. Nanetti, *Making Democracy Work: Civic Traditions in Modern Italy* (Princeton: Princeton University Press, 1993).

12. Marcel Mauss, *The Gift: Forms and Functions of Exchange in Archaic Societies* (New York: Norton, 1967). See also Francis Fukuyama, *Trust: Social Virtues and the Creation of Prosperity* (New York: Free Press, 1995).
13. Abraham Lincoln, "To the People of Sangamo County," March 9, 1832, in *Speeches and Writings*, vol. 1, ed. Don Fehrenbacher (New York: Library of America, 1989), p. 4.
14. Lorraine Smith Pangle and Thomas L. Pangle, *The Learning of Liberty: The Educational Ideas of the American Founders* (Lawrence: University Press of Kansas, 1993).
15. Richard Weaver, *The Ethics of Rhetoric* (South Bend, Ind.: Regnery/Gateway, 1953), p. 112.
16. For notions of what students need to know, see, for example, Benjamin R. Barber and Richard M. Battistoni, eds., *Education for Democracy: Citizenship, Community, Service* (Dubuque, Iowa: Kendall/Hunt, 1993). For notions of what the students' teachers need to know, see Roger Soder, "Teaching the Teachers of the People," in *Democracy, Education, and the Schools*, ed. Roger Soder (San Francisco: Jossey-Bass, 1996), pp. 244–74.

Part Two

Conversations

Chapter Seven

Education for Civility and Civitas

Panel Discussion

Participants:

Benjamin R. Barber (BB)
Linda Darling-Hammond (LDH)
Gary D Fenstermacher (GF)
John I. Goodlad (JG)
Donna H. Kerr (DK)
Theodore R. Sizer (TS)
Roger Soder (RS)

Wednesday, November 1, 1995
Sheraton New York

JG: Let me say at the outset that we do not in any way want to confuse education and schooling. Education is a much deeper, more profound undertaking, done, we hope, in the political entities that are schools serving a purpose in a democratic society.

Every member of this panel is critically concerned about what appears to be the lack or the disappearance of public purpose in our schools. Our schools were created with a public purpose in mind—admittedly a very narrow one—of teaching the principles of religion—a *particular* religion—and the laws of the land. They've had to grow to encompass a much broader public purpose. Now, of course, we hear a great deal about their private purpose: "What are the schools going to do for *me?* What are they going to do to provide me with a better living?" And the national reform rhetoric has been an economic rhetoric, primarily, of international, global economic competition and, in turn, putting more dollars in the individual purse.

We are concerned about the degree to which the schools have a particular role to play in educating the young—not just schooling them, but educating the young—for active participation in a social and political democracy. This means, on one hand, civility in regard to all human relationships and, on the other, contributing to the creation of civitas: an organized political entity that takes care of its business well.

In the preliminary paper that Gary Fenstermacher wrote, he referred to his own experience in growing up and the degree to which the family had provided him with a safe haven in which he could do things and say things that would not be so readily handled in public. He refers to the "in here" and the "out there." What do you mean by that, Gary?

GF: I was trying to determine how it was that we came to this distinction between public and private in our own lives, and I recalled my childhood, when my mother would say to me, "Such things are not done in public," or I would be having a conversation with my father, and he would frown and say, "*[clearing his throat for emphasis]* I hope that won't become public." And it occurred to me as I thought about these things that I had never once asked: "What's the public?" It was part of the rearing, the upbringing of all of us as children that there were things that were done on one side of the front porch, and different things that were done on the other side. What was done in the family became the private world. We talked, not often and not very much, about my father's salary, and how the money got spent. But that conversation wasn't to be repeated when we stepped off the front porch. Or we'd talk about zany or "difficult" relatives; that conversation, too, was not to be repeated as one walked off the front porch.

But there were other kinds of things that one had to learn when one did step off the front porch: that one wasn't automatically loved and cared for and nurtured in this environment beyond one's porch. Therefore, you had to be careful and you had to think and you had to regard people differently. If you were to say something careless, you could hurt and not be readily forgiven, whereas in the home you were entitled to a kind of carelessness, and you might even be loved in spite of being occasionally hurtful. But out there, in that public arena, that wasn't necessarily the case, so a different kind of conduct was required for the public.

I began to wonder whether this distinction between public and private hasn't disappeared in contemporary American society: that what we see in film, on video, on the streets of New York and in other places—the kinds of things that would have previously been condemned in public—now seem to be part of that public arena. I thought about Richard Sennett's book, *The Fall of Public Man,* in which he argued that that which is private seems to have "leaked over" and contaminated that which is public.[1]

And on thinking about this, I noted how many people on this panel, and others, had talked about the notion of restoring a public in American society, and about the role of the public schools in the creation or the renewal of the public. I subscribe to these ideas wholeheartedly. But, at the same time, it occurs to me that we're overlooking the private while we're talking about the restoration or renewal of the public, and that we may think that the public can be restored in the absence of a healthy private. I began to wonder whether, as educators, we don't need to be as attentive to the restoration of the private life that makes public life possible as we are to the public life. The possibility of the disappearance of the distinction between "in here," on one side of the front porch, and "out there," on the other side, leads me to believe that if we're going to restore one, we need to look to restoring both.

JG: Gary, later on in this discussion, near the end, I would like to return to this idea and ask you: when you say that as educators we have to pay more attention to the private, what does that mean? But meanwhile, what about adding to or disagreeing with what Gary had to say?

DK: Gary, I'm really empathic with your pointing to the family as a safe haven. If that's what family and private world mean, then that's wonderful, and maybe it should be promoted. But we also need to recognize that not for everyone has the family—has the private space—been a safe haven. I'm thinking here of possible alternatives. Ray Oldenburg's *The Great Good Place* talks about third places, neither the private world of the home nor the public world of the workplace but something different: a safe haven where strangers might meet.[2] I wonder if you'd respond to that.

GF: They might have been John's words—"safe haven"—and while I think that there's some sense in which family has to play that role, I think of the private, the family, as a kind of primary association where limits were set and I didn't necessarily participate in setting them. Morality was developed without discussion of whether this was a good thing or a bad thing to do, and so what I was attempting to do in my paper was to distinguish this private world, where certain kinds of things occur around a notion of primary associations, from the public world. I think that the private world is better when it's a safe haven, but I'm not so sure that's the essential condition for it.

BB: I don't know if the disruption of traditional boundaries between public and private can be denied. I think you're right to say that there's a major change in how we view public and private. But it seems to me that even in your own conception of it you're talking about the tainting of the public by the private—in a certain sense the corruption of the public by the private—and I would argue that in addition to that, we have the privatization of a lot of things that, in fact, have been public.

You raise a lot of questions. In a way, the question that John asked needs perhaps to be answered now: what does this mean educationally? Currently, a lot of young Americans don't have families to turn to, and if you refer to other primary associations for those children, I don't know what those are. Gangs, maybe? Certainly not churches or synagogues for many young Americans.

One of the problems schools face is that they have become the social institutions of last resort for a host of activities that go well beyond traditional schooling, and even beyond the broader gauge of education. They have become, in some sense, the last surviving public institutions in cities and towns that have been bereft of publicness altogether. Consequently, there's a tremendous burden on them.

Several of the papers looked back to the restoration and reconstitution of the private as a way, perhaps, of trying to save the public, but it seems to me that that plays into the political current of our time, which somehow assumes that the private sphere and markets can do what constituted public institutions cannot do. I think we need to question that deeply. The development of character at home, the development of safe havens, the development of primary institutions is, of course, a *sine qua non* of long-term democratic institutions. But we have to look at what we actually have available to us in the way of schooling and education in that arena. That we should perhaps put public schools in the private arena along with the other bereft and corrupted private institutions of the family and the church and try to get them to do the job seems to me to have the thing wrong way around. My own belief is—and here is maybe the nub of the contest or disagreement on the panel—that it is through the constitution and reconstitution of the public that we can begin to get at the problems that afflict the private realm. That we can somehow go back to moral character and disappearing families and—in the secular society—churches, and hope that by reconstituting them we will create a climate in which public education will follow its own course, though a sweet dream, is politically very unlikely.

GF: Both of you have put the rubber on the road very quickly. This an extraordinarily vexing problem. The notion of separation of church and state, for example, to me, is to draw a line of difference between public and private. Now when we talk about whether by restoring a public we're also making it possible to restore a private, I don't understand what we're driving at. We need institutions in society that nurture and care absent the vote, that aren't public, that lay down groundwork and ground rules. But we need other institutions in society where these are debated and discussed and voted on. I just worry about mixing these two critical functions.

JG: Linda, your paper gets very much into this interaction between this family-developed civility, if you will, and this larger public, and you make the statement: "Freedom is possible only when people come together in a life consciously lived in common." Does that have any bearing on what these people are talking about?

LDH: Yes. I was wending my way through this issue by struggling to understand what it takes to create a people when we say "We the people." The founding fathers mostly made that up. "The people" didn't really exist at that point and, in fact, the founding fathers were just a bunch of guys in Philadelphia—fairly wealthy white guys at that *[Laughter.]*—who hypothesized a people, and then they set out to create one. When you ask the questions "Well, how do you create a people? How do you educate people for self-rule and for shared living?" there are two things we must do: make wise decisions about the public space and live together in some fashion. The capacity of the people for both wisdom and for good behavior together is at the core of the capacity of a democracy to sustain itself. When Hamilton was arguing against the idea of real democracy—that is, one person, one vote—he said to Jefferson, "Thy people, sir, are a beast," and that was enough to carry the thesis that you couldn't trust the people for self-rule. Jefferson's response was to invent the idea of public education: a space where you could build this people.

And in that space there are two kinds of knowledge that we have to be concerned about. One is the kind of thinking that enables people to reason out things for themselves, to figure out what they think to be critical, to evaluate: a kind of learning that is not passive and not rote but very engaged and very much pointed toward critical capacity. But we also need social learning. We also need a place where people learn to understand one another and live together, and do that not just civilly, not just politely, but also with true understanding of one another.

The struggle that we have in schools now to create those two kinds of learning is related to the kind of bureaucratic institution we have evolved over the last century, in which decisions are made at the top of a system by experts or others and handed down rather than debated and made by the people engaged in them, and by a kind of structure for schooling in which students are divided, by their presumed capacity to learn, in tracks and courses that say "You can't be educated with one another. You can't be in common discourse with one another." And it's that that I was referring to when I said "a consciously created common space" where we really work at learning how to understand who we are together as opposed to who we are in our private spaces. In a way, it's bringing some of the private into the public space to allow us to honor and legitimize the experiences each of us has had privately, rather than creating a public space that is artificially civil because it has only a singular point of view or a dominant perspective, which everyone at least ostensibly adheres to.

JG: Roger, in your paper you took a dim view of the surrounding society in regard to its promotion of the education required for Linda's position. But you also took a dim view of the degree to which schools provide the education that's needed. Is there a pony anywhere in this manure pile?

RS: There are many dim views, maybe. I have several dim views that I'd like to share. *[Laughter.]* One is that we have a lot of phrases and mantras that make us feel very comfortable. One of those that you've all heard from every education governor—and every governor wants to be one of those—is the mantra "All children can learn." It makes us feel very good and supposedly gives us our marching orders. The trouble is that in looking at one child we can say, "This person here is going to end up in the mail room of life and therefore only really needs ninth-grade math, whereas this person over here is going to go on to Wharton and do very well, and therefore this person needs calculus and all of that other advanced math. Now, we could say, "All children can learn." But that begs the question: What do you really want children to learn? Because what's operating here is a notion that what you will be in the future determines what you are today. Looking at that one child and saying, "She will go nowhere further than here," or another child, "She will go over here" determines what they will be right now. And we have systematically denied education to a lot of children simply on the basis of saying that all children can learn.

But beyond that, there's a larger question. I'm reminded of a cartoon—I think it was in the *Saturday Review*—that shows two wealthy people looking at some teenagers hanging out, and one says to the other: "When you think of the awesome power of television to educate, aren't you awfully glad it doesn't?"

JG: Ted, I'm pretty sure this issue touches on you. . . .

TS: Oh yes. Television educates, with all due respect to the two people in the cartoon.

You wonder: why is the rhetoric so ferocious among the political estate these days, and the performance so minimal? I think it may be more than just the selfishness of the time. It may mean that the political leadership, the business leadership of the country, has concluded that schools really don't make that much difference, that they keep the kids off the streets, at least when they're little, and teach them how to read, write, and cipher, but other things are influencing them far more than the schools: other institutions. When you look at the research record of how adolescents spend their time and what they think about the time they spend, you have to agree with the political view that, really, public education, private education, any kind of formal education at the elementary and secondary level has relatively little leverage on the intelligence of the people.

It's a sobering thought that people may conclude this. But you listen to what people say and then you watch what they do. And we should listen less to governors and look more at their budgets. And then, looking at their budgets, say: "What does that say about the assumptions behind those budgets?" I think that our influence in schools is increasingly meager. Schools don't deliver on these promises for civitas and high learning and high standards. Quietly, people understand that that's the case, so they say: "Don't give it much money. Other institutions are going to be, and already are, more important." So I go back to John's point: education is a lot more than schooling, perhaps never more in this century than now. The educating influences in the information-rich culture that is ours are increasingly and very rapidly growing, drawn from outside the walls of the public schools.

JG: Benjamin Barber touches on this issue in two papers of his: one that argues that the workplace undoes each day what the school day does, and then the one for this symposium that addresses the issue of waste and what we're prepared to waste money on. Want to plow into either of those or both?

BB: Let me just say a quick word about the second and then address the first because it responds directly to Ted. There's a lot of talk about wastage, and I simply point out that if you want to see what a society really values, look at what it's willing to waste a little money on. When it comes to defense spending, there are no limits on the possible wastage, and most people would say, "Well, that's all right. If we waste a little, we'll have security. We really want security; we need it. Let's waste a little." When the schools spend ten cents more than they're supposed to, all the accountants are out there adding up the budgets and saying, "Wow, you people are really wasting money." Norman Mailer tells a story in a recent article of his. When he ran for mayor of this city back in the 1960s, he was talking to some people who were receiving welfare. One mother got up and walked out of the meeting, saying, "Look, all I want is a share of the waste for us." Maybe the plea that school superintendents and others should make is "How about a little of America's waste being sent our way for a change instead of holding us to high budgetary and accounting standards?" while every other budget in areas people care about—say, television programs—is not held to the same high standards. It is an elaboration on Ted's notion: don't just look at budgets, look at where we're willing to waste some money, and then you'll see what a country really values.

But I want to respond directly to Ted because he was saying two things, and I think they're a little different. On the one hand, he was saying there are rival tutors to schooling in America. Tocqueville talked about an immense tutelary power set up over a democratic society. And once upon a time, I think we thought that our schools constituted that immense tutelary power—the tutor of the whole nation. Now I think we could all probably agree that television is that tutor. It has the kids seven days a week, six hours a day, fifty-two weeks a year, instead of four or five hours a day, five days a week for twenty or thirty weeks a year, at best.

But part of what Ted was saying was that the country knows that the education they get from the rivals is actually better and more effective and teaches what they need to know, and so we don't really need schools, so why pay for them? And, of course, part of the problem is that what the rival tutor, television, is telling us is precisely that schooling *isn't* necessary. It doesn't say that in its preachments and its mantras, but it says that in the values it conveys. Where in a modern television program—even on public television—do you really get the sense that knowing something about the Civil War or having read Plutarch or being familiar with the poems of Emily Dickinson is going to get you ahead in this society? When you watch television, what you should be persuaded of is that if you have a rubber arm or a golden larynx you can make a lot of money, and that's a good thing; or if you're fast with figures or have a loud voice in the pits down on Wall Street, if you can get your orders in fast, you can make a lot of money in the commodities market. The things that our society says it cares about in the values it displays are very different from the mantras that it goes through when it's talking about education and the public purposes of education.

My argument is that our kids are smart, not stupid, in reading that lesson. They have a nose for hypocrisy. They see what the country cares about. They can tell by budgets and wastage and the values on TV what it really cares about, and when they don't take their own schooling seriously—and a lot of parents don't take it seriously—they're actually reading the country right, not wrong. We throw up our hands and say: "Don't they see how important education is?" They see exactly how important it is, which is *not at all* if you look at the other clues, the other signals that are coming from the wider, commercial society. And that's the way in which the rival tutors of television and the market make their message. Unfortunately, it's a message that undoes all of the high ideals of public education that we talk about at conferences like this.

TS: Commerce depends on an unsophisticated audience. Not only do the commercial media dominate the culture, they also depend on an undiscriminating viewer. So you lose on two counts.

DK: I think the way we talk about education and schooling gets us a little bit confused and in trouble. It might help us understand why kids can see that we don't take schooling or education very seriously. The confusion goes something like this: we tend to talk about education as being instrumental to building a democracy. What do we do? Generally, we say that if we could just get the kids to have enough knowledge and skills about how to run the machinery of a democracy, if we could get everyone schooled so that it would be possible for them to make a real contribution to the society, if we could also get everyone so well educated or highly skilled that the nation could compete well in the world, and if we could build the schools as strong communities, then we would have made the connection between education and democracy.

But you could do *all* of those things and still that would not block the nemesis of democracy, that is, relationships of domination and subservience. You could have highly skilled people and a very undemocratic society. You could have everyone skilled to make contributions but those contributions, those possibilities, not received well. We could have a nation that's at the top of the world and dominant and still an ugly nation. We could have communities that, in fact, don't promote democratic relationships; history is full of such communities.

So what is it we're jumping over? I think we get in trouble when we ask: "What do we want our children to learn?" when we're thinking about education and democracy. We need to start with a different question, and that is: "How is it we want ourselves to stand in relationship to one another?" If the answer is that we want to stand in democratic relationships, in relationships of mutuality, then we have a somewhat different task.

And I don't say this to point the finger. I'll share a story with you that's in my paper. I found myself not too long ago in a line at an airport in San Francisco, waiting for the shuttle back to Seattle. In front of me was a young woman, probably mid-twenties, with neon carrot color hair, very, very short hair, dressed totally in black: black leather jacket over a black halter, black tights, black combat boots, studs in her nose and ears. I caught myself—and I was very uncomfortable with this—casting her as foreign to me, as "the other." For a moment there, how was I standing in relation to her? Well, there are ways to check ourselves and sense the human solidarity.

But what happens if I continue to see her as "the other"? If you're not me, then who are you? Are you someone I need to control? Are you someone I need to "fix"? Is it that I need to be a part of rehabilitating, fixing, schooling this young woman who's in front of me? And if the rehabilitation doesn't work, then do I maybe need to start blaming her for things that bother me much as Henry Ford blamed the Jews for just about everything that bothered Henry Ford?

So there's a lot at stake here. And I think the fundamental issue is: how do we want to stand in relationship to one another? That's the fundamental question, that's why we seek a democracy, because if we have a commitment to democratic relations it's got to be in the relationships themselves.

LDH: I think that that configuration of the question really poses for us the issue of building education not so much *for* democracy but education *as* democracy. It's the question of *how*—and I'd like to think about this in schools, although that's not the only place to think about it—we build a common space for shared living in which we really come to understand one another, not as "the other," but as connected and able to appreciate one another in fundamental ways.

And I think that that raises for us the real, serious dilemma that within the democratic society, schools may conduct themselves as the least democratic institutions. They are frequently, perhaps predominantly, authoritarian institutions. The relations in them are structured such that there are rules created that are frequently—more or less explicitly—enforced differentially for kids who have been put in relation to one another as different. There are the smart kids and the dumb kids. They're streamed differently. There are the good kids and the bad kids. Not only do they come to know how they are labeled, but quite often administrators enforce those distinctions. I was at a high school recently where a set of fairly draconian and trivial rules was being enforced in ways that put lots of children of color in detention regularly. A minute late to class here, a small violation there; wearing Band-Aids is an offense. You name it. There are ways that people's places in society are reinforced by virtue of all of the trivial violations that they can make. A high-status kid got caught in one of these violations, and the parent was told: "Well, that enforcement shouldn't have happened. That child is one of the good kids." Good kids don't receive the penalties that are widely dispensed to the others. That's not unusual. And we have to think through the issue of how schools can have the conditions of size, of relation of people to one another, of commitments that allow them to enact democracy.

DK: I find very persuasive Jessica Benjamin's work on what happens when human beings, as we do, simultaneously have the need for independence and recognition. Here's the problem: You're out of my control and I still need your recognition. If that's resolved on the side of domination, I'm going to control you so I'll get your recognition. If we resolve it on the side of being subservient, we say: "I'll be subservient to you so I can get your recognition." The democratic resolution is very, very different from that. It's a giving of mutual recognition; it's not easy to come by.

LDH: And the reality for school practitioners is that if you say, "Here's a group of three thousand kids in a building that you have to make learning occur for," it's very difficult to resolve questions of relationships in ways that allow for a resolution different from the ones that you posed.

DK: That's where the power of Benjamin Barber's point comes in, that we maybe need to be willing to waste some resources on human beings, that we need to have adults who are self-responsible and responsive "hanging out" with kids. And that's not with 150 kids passing through every day. But maybe we need some of that wastage.

BB: Could I just link Donna's point to the point earlier about public and private? Because I think there is a connection, and we need to see it. It's been the dream of idealists at least from the beginning of time that we would find ways to create equality in the private relations of men and women and blacks and whites, and through those private relations create a model of public relations, social relations, and civic relations. But, in fact, for very good reasons, that's not how it's happened, and I don't think it's how it should happen. In that sense I disagree tactically with the therapeutic approach to "the other" and the individual as an approach that can really deal with issues of inequality. We don't want to deal with inequality in the private realm, because the only way you can deal with inequality in the private realm is to encroach on the private realm, order and regulate relations there in a totalitarian fashion, and create egalitarianism.

That's what the public realm is for. The public realm is a civic realm where we—through regulation, social relations, law, politics, and citizenship—create relations of equality that then can, at a distance, regulate and prevent abuses in the private realm. But I don't think it's a good idea that we create a situation in which we put the burden on the private realm to overcome inequality by dealing therapeutically with issues of self and other and trying to create young Americans who all love and respect each other. I'd much rather say to them: "You can think what you want about one another to a point in the private realm. You can have your clubs. You can write and express yourself, and you might use language that is offensive. But you are also citizens of a common school, a common neighborhood, a common nation, and a common globe. And in your civic participation as members, there *are* rules, there are important issues of equality, and it's there that we will take them up."

But it's an old argument in America: do we start privately and create equality there, and then create a foundation for public equality, or do we use our public institutions to create a public skein of equality, which then makes possible the regulation of inequality without massive interference and disruption and encroachment on our liberties?

DK: Benjamin, I couldn't agree more with the analytical point, but I couldn't disagree more with the practical point. Is it public or private realm when, as Valerie Polakow describes in elementary school classrooms, there are certain kids whose experience is not even given credence? Who are treated in ways that certainly are dominating? Is this public or private realm?

BB: Linda's position, I think, is a mediator between ours because what Linda said, I really agree with: schools themselves as public institutions have to embody democratic civic and social relations. There's a real sense that you're saying: "Schools and the public domain aren't where equality is going to happen until we face up to issues of equality in our individual relations between self and other." What I'm saying is: I think *that* is a pipe dream. That's unlikely to happen. To the extent that we try to make schools also teach lessons about individual relations, that's fine, because that's happening in the public domain of schooling. So it's tactical issues, I think, that separate us.

DK: One last comment on this. I think where we're talking about matters of character, we're talking not just private, but also public. Character has the two aspects. One might call part of it, the more private part, the "soul," the "tending of the soul"; but there's also character as a stance toward the soul and how one is in the world. When we think of great characters we think of people who act in the world in certain ways. These are public matters.

BB: The danger, Donna, is that "Soviet man" is also a characterological ideal. The Soviet state had a very clear notion of what a good human being was, and tried to impose it. I worry, when you begin talking characterologically about these issues, that you invite the state and public institutions to begin to come in and mold human character. And while it may be a character that's more egalitarian, it's not one that I look forward to seeing in this country.

DK: There's a big difference, though, in taking characterological features off a notion of the good that's put upon people rather than one that comes from the people and looks at mode and manner of standing in relationship to others.

JG: Roger, you've been trying to get into this discussion. . . .

RS: Donna and I have talked about some of these matters before, and I imagine we will continue talking about them. I would argue that, if you're going to have citizens functioning effectively in a democracy, there are some things that they have to know about and appreciate in terms of equity issues and due process of law: some fundamental aspects of a democracy. If you're arguing that that sort of knowledge is not sufficient in order to have a democracy, then I could turn the same question back to you. I can't see, necessarily, where your position is sufficient, either, because I don't see how knowledge of the kind you're talking about will lead to some sense of what Ralph Lerner said makes a political regime actual, that is to say, "the institutions, procedures, and habits of mind." So I'm not excluding that, but I just don't see that that can necessarily get us to where we need to get by itself.

DK: What I'm wanting to say is that education understood as instrumental to democracy is important, but there are issues of human solidarity and how we stand in relationship to one another that are also essential. So I'm not wanting to argue that either is sufficient by itself.

JG: I want to cycle back here and begin the shift toward the positive kinds of things that can be done in the face of this array of circumstances we're talking about. I want to go back, Linda, to your critique of the way in which the systemics of schooling lay onto the school and the classroom and the problems this creates. I reflect on Ted's paper for this symposium, in which he talks about the fact that children don't really have access to *public schooling*, they have access to *one public school*, so it's not really public access. It sounds to me as though, if these arguments are developed enough, we are giving strong ammunition to the people whose material is coming across my desk these days and who are referring not to the separation of church and state, but to the separation of school and state. They are talking about teachers prepared under state requirements, textbooks prescribed by the state, and so on, and they're saying: "Enough already. Get rid of this public system of schooling." And it sounds to me as though our condemnation of this system is leading into the hands of those who are saying: "We don't need a public school."

LDH: I think that this is, at another level, the same issue of education *as* democracy. We have created a system, which we call a public education system, that has substantially operated on principles of coercion. That is, you go to the school that is in your neighborhood, and if you're not a wealthy person, you may not have a choice of neighborhood or a choice of school. You are subject to the way in which that school behaves, which in some cases is dehumanizing and inhumane and harmful to children. We say it must be done "thus and so." With an intention to ensure certain kinds of things, we've layered on elements of coercion in public schooling that I think are unnecessary and, in fact, counterproductive to the spirit of public education. And we've done that in grossly unequal ways, covering our eyes to the extent to which the public school to which one has access is radically different if one lives in the South Bronx or if one lives in Scarsdale or New Rochelle or any other community that has a different property-tax base or set of ideas and commitments about education. In order to preserve the spirit and intention of public education, we've got to figure out what elements of coercion can be let go of, and where we can allow for choice. Where, in fact, the public purposes of public schooling are sufficiently clear and compelling, there may be some common core of experiences that we want to ensure remain in schools that then are open to choices.

In doing that, we've also got to confront the inequality issue much more explicitly than we have. In this country, a recent report from NCES *[National Center for Education Statistics]* points out, we have schools that spend one thousand dollars a year per student and schools that spend fifty thousand dollars a year. Those are obviously the far extremes, but it is *not* unusual in any given state for one set of schools to be spending two or three times what others can, operating with highly able staffs, teachers, and materials, and others functioning with personnel who are untrained, unable to meet the demands for the kinds of knowledge that we think students should have access to, not to mention the kinds of settings in which they can be supported in a real, genuine learning opportunity.

TS: This word "choice" is a critical one, and a lot of current defenders of public education as it is say, "Well, 'choice' is the neoconservative or the conservative banner." I don't think we should assert who owns the notion. It's a fundamental notion in a democracy, it seems to me. The word "public" means "open access," and public education does not have open access unless you're rich. If you have enough money to move from the South Bronx to Scarsdale, to take the local example, you're quite free to do that. And many of us picked the communities in which we purchased houses on the basis of the quality of the public schools. Not only did we have the initial money for the down payment on the mortgage, but the federal government gave us the subsidy of allowing us to deduct the interest on that mortgage from our income taxes. So we were, indeed, underwritten by public law in the exercise of our choice.

A lot of families in this country do not have choice. As a result, American public schools—public schools, the great common school, the bringer together of all the people—are, in fact, profoundly segregated by class. Until we face that, until we say "If choice is good for some folks, it's good for all folks" and "What are the public policies necessary to make public education as open as public transit systems are?" we kid ourselves.

JG: The implication? The implication then being that instead of being able to take our tax dollars to help pay for the school of choice I already have my children in, we need to pay more tax dollars in order to ensure greater equity among the schools from which people can choose so that the schools are so commonly good that the choice won't be so critical?

LDH: I love the idea of the schools being commonly good.

JG: But isn't that a built-in necessity—that they have to be commonly good? The Achilles' heel of the liberal movement is the distribution of wealth. No question about it. It's never been seriously addressed because it's too volatile. And it's not being seriously addressed now. That is part of the tension at the present time. But here we're saying, I think, that in order to provide the public school within which a public purpose will be attained, we need to ensure that the schools, to the best of our knowledge, have the conditions that will make it possible for children to enjoy the kind of learning that we would probably agree upon here. Then the matter of whether or not you can get across town to another school doesn't matter so much. In fact, it might be a disadvantage because you now lose your community if you have one.

So, in essence, are we saying that we have a civic responsibility to maintain a public system of schooling in which there is, to the extent possible, equity? That is running quite counter to the current rhetoric about schooling in our society, which is saying: "Look, the schools are bureaucratic, the teachers are prepared bureaucratically, the regulations are bureaucratic, indeed, compulsory schooling is bureaucratic."

GF: I think we're all puzzled by the distinction between what we *want* and what *is* or what's going to happen. On the one hand we sit here and praise democracy, and on the other hand we're unhappy with the decisions that seem to be made in one. It's possible that the public school is gone, and that we're just at the beginning of the wake. If I read tea leaves one way, they're finished. We're looking at choice, we're looking at privatization, and if we're looking for a tactical orientation, the question is how to preserve a public if we depend on or have depended on public schools in the past to create some concept of public. (I don't think that schools were ever the progenitors of the public, but as Tom Green would say, they were the instruments of it: they don't make it happen, they sustain it when it's already there.) So if we think about this possibility that what, as educators, we're committed to is the maintenance of this distinction between private and public life, and that if we care about democracy we care about having mechanisms in society to continue this notion of public, of civitas, of civility, how are we going to do that when the nature of schooling in America is changing before our very eyes? And that may be the question rather than what feels, anyway, to be a little reactionary: that is, how do we save this system that I'm not sure ever did what we keep thinking it does?

TS: With the system, we've always had choice—as long as we're wealthy. One of the happy sides of the current howling and screaming in education policy is that some things that were unsayable are now sayable. And we put up the mirror. We say, "What's public education?" Well, public education is designed around people who have resources. And that's the way it works. It's always worked that way.

GF: Isn't it the case, though, when you listen to people who want vouchers, they are often not wealthy, and they believe that this is a way for them to get a hold of the brass ring?

TS: That's right. It is folks who couldn't move to Scarsdale *[saying]*, "Give me the money the way my uncle got it with the G.I. Bill."

GF: So, in a sense, choice is seen by many as a provision for equity.

TS: Exactly. And it could be, if it's defined in a certain way, just as the bureaucratically run public education system now could be if it were defined in a certain way.

GF: So, might we not concentrate our energies and intellectual talents in that direction?

TS: Indeed. And it's very scary—

GF: I agree.

TS: But it's also full of opportunity. That's why the shaping of the proposition in California on vouchers is so important, why people like Jack Coons are so important: for being smart lawyers and philosophers who have thought about these things, so, whatever we do, it isn't mindless. But we have to get away from the labels: that's conservative, that's liberal, that's a Republican thing, that's a Democratic thing. Forget that stuff, and go back as we're doing in this symposium to the basics. What is democracy? And who decides?

We keep talking, all of us, myself included, about "we." "We need this or we need that." Who are *we?* And by what right do we prescribe for Johann's kids?

LDH: Let me just add one principle, or perhaps it's a distinction, with respect to the conversation about choice and democracy. First of all, choice does not necessarily equal privatization. One can think about choice in the public sphere, which is not always how it's thought about.

But John raised for us a fundamental point that I don't want us to gloss by. He said: "What if we had schools that were commonly good?" That is to say, what if we made the decision that most democracies have made: that schools will be equally funded? Period. That's just the basis for school funding in most other social democracies. And then said, "Let's figure out, once schools have equal resources, what it is that they'll do." We have made exactly the opposite decision. We have funded them grossly unequally, and then we've tried to create a presumption of equality by regulating them and saying, "You all are now the same. You must adopt the same textbooks, you must follow the same curriculum," and so on. So we have precluded choice about almost all of the important aspects of teaching and learning in the name of equity, without providing the resources that would allow for schools to be commonly good.

GF: I love that idea. But what I want to say about public and private is: no one side is good unless the other side is. It's possible to have equally funded schools and a set of parents who don't have a decent job. And, lacking a decent job, they lack the kind of dignity to bring to home life that would enable children to come to school ready to benefit from common funding. What I care about is working both sides of the line, so that if we do have equally funded schools, which I think is a terrific ideal, we have children in them who can benefit from them.

LDH: How do you work the other side of the line?

GF: *[Sighs.]* How do you work the other side of the line? This is the question that John said he was going to ask me, isn't it? *[Laughs.]*

JG: It's close!

GF: Benjamin Barber talked about how tricky it is and, when he was taking some reservation to what Donna was saying, worried about the idea of the state getting in the business of telling what was good in the private realm: this notion of the Soviet man. That's what bugs us all.

And so, with that caveat, let me mention a few things. I dislike, for example, the way the Right puts down the Left and the Left puts down the Right in this society: when the Religious Right makes an appeal, or a Dan Quayle makes an appeal for family values, and the Liberal Left just thinks it's like Gerald Ford banging his head on a helicopter, and everybody laughs. I think the first step is seeing that when people ask for things, they may not know how to achieve them or precisely what they are, but it's important to value and respect that they're needy and they're looking for something. We have to stop playing the political game the way we're playing it. I don't know how to do that, but it's an improvement in public life that I think would benefit private life. I think of Stephen Carter's book, *The Culture of Disbelief*, when he's talking about how publicly we have "dissed" religion in our society, and what the problems are with doing that.[3] It makes it very hard to sustain religion in the private arena when it gets dissed so heavily in the public.

I don't believe in censorship any more than most others do, but I sympathize with the task of parents who are raising children today when the public arena has almost no standards for what makes acceptable discourse, acceptable visual imagery, or anything else.

And, I think, again, jobs are important, work is important, income is important to build private opportunity and decent private spaces; people are entitled to the dignity that comes from good work, and that affects how they deal with their children.

BB: Gary, that's very fair, and I think you've outlined an important series of issues. But you've also put education, properly, back into the larger political context. I would feel a lot better if we were saying: "Let's have more choice in education." But I would also feel better if we lived in a society that was saying genuinely: "Until we get things straight in the family and in the churches and in the private realm, anything we do in the schools isn't much going to count, so let's downgrade and defund the schools a little bit. Let's have some vouchers and more choice in schools. And we're going to put all our energies and resources into really taking hold of and doing something for the failing institutions of church, family, and all the other social agencies, social and civil institutions, that aren't working." But we're not doing that. We're defunding right across the board. We're privatizing there, too. We're saying, "Let welfare mothers take care of themselves." We're not putting more funding, more help, more assistance in other areas while we're saying "Gee, maybe the schools just can't do it all; maybe we're asking too much of the schools; let's downgrade them a little and upgrade the social agenda for these other institutions." The folks who are defunding the schools and saying, "The schools can't do it all; let's go back to family values," are not putting their money where their mouths are, are not "wasting" any money—to use my language again—on those areas. So, frankly, there's a certain degree of hypocrisy in the political agenda that is out there.

The larger issue is that it's true that we need choice in public education. We need ways to find it, and part of the frustration of some people who begin to look at vouchers and privatization is that they think it will give them more choice. We have to ask, are there ways to get more choice into the public system—with charter schools and other things? And obviously there are. But choice isn't the only value. Choice isn't the only thing education is concerned with. Choice is a parameter associated with the liberty side of these things. But when you associate the equality side or the community side, there are other values we're after, and other goals we're after. Even if you could make the argument that, on the whole, privatization and vouchers do better by choice in this climate than any reforms that public education can do, you do that at the cost of all the *other* things that public education can do that privatization and vouchers cannot do, which include common schools and democratic education. The danger of privatization is that it allows people to fall back into, in effect, educational clubs for people just like them. So I think we can't just make the sole measure of education reform and the decision about vouchers whether choice is treated well or not; we have to balance choice against other things. Put in that balance, and given that there are ways in which educational reform in the public domain can take account of choice, it seems to me that we'd do much better to look for ways to repair and change public education to make it more choice-oriented than to give up the public school ship, and say "Well, it doesn't do choice very well, so let's really go with choice and go to privatization" and then give up all the other things that public schooling can do.

TS: I completely agree with that. How it's done is, for me, crucial. To re-regulate so you've got choice between Tweedledum and Tweedledee, to say "We'll control the goals, standards, tests, and everything, and you can do what you want" misses the point. Choice has to be real.

It's considered naive these days, but I believe the essence of democracy is persuasion. I think a powerful bit of public discourse about what are the qualities of good public schools is a far healthier route for democracy than re-regulating a system of choice.

JG: As we get into the kind of thing we're talking about now, I think there is something that we need to recognize, which might be that strange, larger atmosphere that seems to exist at certain periods in time, when a lot of things could happen or are happening, and yet we don't quite see the connection. But if you look around right now, you see a lot of people reaching out for something better. Seymour Sarason talks about this quite a bit, referring to the need for community and the need for a "sense of the sacred." And he says, as the feeling of loss of community increases, the push toward the sacred and the divine also increases. That helps explain some of the reaching out for divine guidance right now when people are very disturbed about the lack of secular guidance. I think that it is time for us as educators to begin to capitalize on some of this desire before it could go the other way.

On a recent television news program, someone took this argument we're hearing here about increased poverty, one child in twelve hungry, only about a third of our society prepared to take advantage of the educational system, and so on. These things were addressed to a very visible political figure, and he was asked, "What's going to be the consequence of this trend that's in our society?" He said, "Revolution." It was a remarkable comment from someone who clearly is acting in ways to reduce the care of our fellow citizens, who at the same time says, "If we go on like this, we're going to have a revolution." It seems almost as though it's a train coming down the track that we're not able to stop.

We're representing here two major programs of educational improvement: the Coalition of Essential Schools and the National Network for Educational Renewal, and I wonder if we are making ourselves heard enough. For example, a member of our staff is Calvin Frazier, whom many of you know. Cal comes out of a responsibility as a state commissioner of education and has had a lot to do with setting state standards; he comes out of that kind of model. But Cal always is our conscience, and he will say, "How is this program going to succeed, when all around us are these other expectations?" And then he sums these up. What they really come down to is the old model of inputs, outputs, and no attention whatsoever to the classroom or the school in between. At a recent dinner, Cal was again enunciating these concerns for our program and saying, "How do we expect to get where we're trying to go under these circumstances?" I said, "Cal, maybe the time has come to say to the policymakers, who have been dealing with a completely outworn model of educational improvement, 'You're wrong. You're using the wrong model.'"

What typically do we do instead? We say, "How do we adjust to this? How, somehow or other, do we make those tests work?" I have met in the last three years in full-day seminars with nearly four hundred school superintendents, about a third of whom can't wait till retirement, about a third of whom are absolutely disillusioned, and about a third of whom still have a little hope. Again and again it comes down to what's being put upon them. When I ask them, "Are you better off because of educational reform since *A Nation At Risk* or worse off?" almost unanimously they say "Worse off." The time has come for us to say, "Enough already." Because we *do know* what a good classroom is like. We *do know* what a good school is like. We *know* those things. And so I'm wondering whether the time has come to quit saying,

"How do we adjust to what we know is not going to get us anywhere, which weakens our effort, and how do we assume a stronger educational voice at the same time?" And how do we join, as Jim Comer has done, for example, very closely with the home in this "in here" and "out there" discussion that Gary started with?

I'll use just one illustration. I don't know if you had time to read the *New York Times* this morning, but if you did, there's a fascinating story in there about the new superintendent of schools in Seattle. We have a military figure, a general, John Stanford, who's superintendent of schools, who worked with Colin Powell in Desert Storm—a major military figure. On being asked by parents, "What are you going to do for our schools?" he turned it around and said, "What are *you* going to do?"

I would say that if we're going to have a public system of schooling that works, with choice and commonly good schools, the schools have to demand something of the participants. I pay taxes for roads, parks, schools, and the like that I don't use. That does not relieve me of paying the taxes or permit me to use the roads, parks, and schools according to my private rules. Indeed, I am not allowed to use the roads and parks as I wish. Nor am I allowed to claim part of them as my own. There is a strong movement in the country right now to treat schools differently—not to pay taxes for them and to privatize them if we do. Without public support and a public sense of responsibility for schools, our system of public education will collapse and so, I fear, will our democracy. Threaten the existence of a public purpose for schooling and you threaten the future existence of democracy.

I think there is, at the present time, a need to articulate this message. I don't think the voice of faith needs higher decibels; I think the voice of reason needs higher decibels, and that's the educational voice. We're a big part of that. And maybe we're too mute.

TS: I'm more optimistic about these things than I was three years ago—five years ago—because I sense, and I'm not alone, a grassroots public education movement under way. It has largely nothing to do with all the stuff that's being talked about.

JG: I agree.

TS: There is loving and respectful disobedience in epidemic quantities in many communities, including this wonderful city. Folks, to put it in the negative, are saying, "We're not gonna take this anymore." But that's not the mood. It's that people are saying, "We can't wait around for the polity to argue this out. We're just gonna do it. And if you don't like it, do something about it." Every day it's easier because more and more kids are demonstrably better served. And the people in the hierarchy mess with schools that work at some political disadvantage. The trick is to give this grassroots movement powers of acceleration and a voice. But it's happening. It's just beginning, but it's there. And the question is: How do you seize this? Heaven knows, grassroots-level initiative on behalf of children is democracy in its purest form.

DK: I think, John, that one of the problems you've identified implicitly has to do with a confusion that if we're concerned about human relationships, that that's therapeutic, so throw it out. That it's not part of the public realm. I think what you're talking about, John, is when schools work well, when a classroom works well, there is a lot of attention to the character of the human relationships. There is a lot of attention to how that classroom relates to the community around it. And those concerns cannot be reduced to education as defined through particular achievement goals. There's much more going on. It has to do with how lives touch one another, with our ability to be responsive to the pain of one another, whether it's students or teachers or community members. We're dealing not just with rules and roles but with human relationships. And I think that's what gets washed out in the talk about particular goals.

LDH: To the extent that we can attend to the quality not only of relationships in classrooms but also the quality and nature of the discourse, we can avoid regulation in the private sphere. Gary gave the example of how distressing it is that people don't hear one another: the far Right can't listen to the Left and the Left can't listen to the Right, and the "dissing" that goes on in the discourse. It's troubling. And yet we don't want to regulate that discourse. We don't want somebody, Big Brother, to come in and say, "Well now, you can't behave that way. You can't talk that way to one another or about one another." We don't want that to be handled through regulation, even though it is distressing. I think the only alternative is to handle it through education of a particular kind. It's the kind of education that goes on in a place like the Urban Academy here in New York City, or Central Park East Secondary School, where one of the foundations of the classroom work is that students explicitly learn to hear one another. They learn that you can say anything, but you can't disrespect someone else's point of view. You have to listen. You have to hear it out. You have to at least try to understand what the person is saying. And that kind of discourse, when it occurs in communities of students that are put together and conducted in a democratic way is, I think, what builds a public that can later conduct its affairs in a manner that needs less regulation because it has more capacity for discourse.

BB: I don't disagree with that at all. But I do think we want to remember that the realm of politics is not just the realm of hearing and consensus and liking people. Actually, it's the realm where we learn to live with our adversaries, our enemies: where we learn to live with conflict.

LDH: That's right.

BB: There's a way in which I think sometimes civic education is conflict averse—maybe because the classroom is conflict averse—that is actually very dangerous to what I regard as good civic education. There is a therapeutic approach to these things that assumes that unless we like each other, a democracy won't work; unless we're friends, a democracy won't work. But, in fact, democracy is a polity of strangers and a polity of antagonists and a polity of people who don't get along, and maybe even don't share fundamental values, but still have to live together and have to find a way other than the gun or the fist to solve and resolve or live with their differences.

JG: I want to thank the members of the panel for what they have had to say, and I think we end on a good note concerning the individual and the polity.

Notes

1. Richard Sennett, *The Fall of Public Man* (New York: Knopf, 1977).
2. Ray Oldenburg, *The Great Good Place: Cafes, Coffee Shops, Community Centers, Beauty Parlors, General Stores, Bars, Hangouts, and How They Get You Through the Day* (New York: Paragon House, 1989).
3. Stephen L. Carter, *The Culture of Disbelief: How American Law and Politics Trivialize Religious Devotion* (New York: Basic Books, 1993).

Chapter Eight

Prospects for Reform

Conversation with the Audience

Participants:

Benjamin R. Barber (BB)
Linda Darling-Hammond (LDH)
Gary D Fenstermacher (GF)
John I. Goodlad (JG)
Donna H. Kerr (DK)
Theodore R. Sizer (TS)
Roger Soder (RS)

Wednesday, November 1, 1995
Sheraton New York

JG: I look back to where we were this morning. Prior to our coming here, each panelist wrote a short paper advancing her or his position. For this symposium, I set a design that moved from the notion that Donna Kerr was developing, which had to do with the self, with the way that we *are* with other people. I use that phrase right out of one of your sentences, Donna, "the way we *are* with other people."

In order to connect the "in here" and "out there," I drew upon Gary Fenstermacher, who had chosen these phrases. I thought that this would be a nice way to ease into the more complicated discussion in which we have engaged this morning.

Linda Darling-Hammond has written lucidly and passionately about the "out there" in regard to the importance of schools that—picking up on my phrase—are "commonly good" in the way they serve their public purpose.

Benjamin Barber has attracted attention recently, particularly for two popular papers: one on how the surrounding society defeats what it is that we want the schools to do by way of public purpose, and then a more recent paper developing the notion of what we mean by "civil societies."[1] He touched on both themes in his earlier remarks.

Ted Sizer raised a different but very related issue by pointing out the degree to which the public school system is one to which not everyone has public access. The prevailing choice options exclude some people.

And Roger Soder took to task both the surrounding context and what goes on within schools. In his work, he is trying to determine what we can do positively in both of these settings.

The idea was to try to move from this depiction of what we think the problems are at the present time to a positive approach regarding what we can do. We were on that theme when we ended the panel discussion. Now we invite you, the audience, to pick up the theme to see if there are questions you might have, short speeches you might want to make, disagreements you might have . . . and so here we will hear from Don Ernst.

Don Ernst: Thank you. My name is Don Ernst. I work now at ASCD *[Association for Supervision and Curriculum Development]*. I'm struck by this conversation after having come from a very difficult conversation with folks who are working with the National Governors' Association on something called Workforce Development, or "School-to-Work." I was one of the only people who I suspect would define himself or herself as a generalist: someone who worries hard about the issues that we've talked about here this morning and about school reform. What was scary to me, in the conversation that occurred in Kansas City with these folks who are concerning themselves with developing standards for work, is that there was absolutely no language, no spirit even, about educating for moral and democratic purposes. Moreover, there was no recognition of this issue, and there were no folks there who knew much about kids in schools.

My point, and I guess it's an observation and a question, is that I'm deeply worried that people with lots of power—governors and others—are pushing school reform agendas without any sense of how schools might address the moral and political dimensions involved in educating our young citizens. I worry that we have two steamships that are sailing away, neither with attention to the other, so that eventually they might crash into one another. I'm worried, on one hand, about how we are going to prevent this. Should we seek to prevent it? How are we going to make connections with those folks who are sailing their ships at full steam and with political authority? I would appreciate your responses or comments.

JG: Gary, your Stanley Elam Lecture last year addressed one of the two issues that Don is raising. That is, surrounding the school reform movement over the last dozen years there has been no mention of educating for the public purpose in a democracy.[2]

GF: I was thinking, Don, while you were raising your question, of Benjamin Barber's line in *An Aristocracy of Everyone*,[3] which I think is derivative in some sense from Tocqueville, that what it takes to live in a democracy is to learn the lessons of liberty, and Benjamin's claim that we just haven't been teaching the lessons of liberty. So it's no surprise that when those people to whom you refer get together to talk about what ought to constitute educational reform, they possess no repertoire whatsoever for being engaged in this kind of discourse. In one sense, I think that what we're doing today is very important: to create a rhetoric or renew or refurbish a rhetoric around these ideas and hope that it will expand. The other alternative is to wait this sucker out. I'm puzzled about how to proceed.

JG: Roger?

RS: Don, one of the things that you expressed concern about is that maybe these political leaders don't understand what they are doing when they get together at these meetings and talk. Another, and dimmer, point of view is that maybe they do know what they're doing. And I go back to a couple of folks. One is Tocqueville, who suggested that if we weren't careful in this country we would end up being nothing more than "a flock of timid and hardworking animals." You might think that that's a bad, reprehensible thing, but I'm wondering whether everybody would think that it's such a bad and reprehensible thing. We can also go back, as I have done several times, to the claim made by the Grand Inquisitor in *The Brothers Karamazov* that people don't want freedom; they want to be ruled by "miracle, mystery, and authority." If we put both of those together, then I think that we have another problem to consider: It's a variation of what I was saying was in that *Saturday Review* cartoon about when you think of the awesome power of television to educate, aren't you awfully glad it doesn't. That is, another question we need to face square on—an antecedent question, before we ask "Should we place more emphasis on the public or the private in doing these things?"—is whether, indeed, there is really all that much of a desire out there for the kind of democracy and freedom that we are talking about.

JG: Were you moving forward to say something, Linda?

LDH: Yes. Actually, your question connects for me to a conversation that Donna and I had during the break. We were talking about how one continues to raise the issues of caring and relationship and the meaning of children's lives for them in a context where the discourse is all about standards and raising the bar, sorting more effectively those who have done or can do from those who have not and cannot and therefore will be decertified from other opportunities. I think the workplace prep conversation is very much one of those. A task force that I'm currently a member of is having that same conversation now around primary grades education. There's a strong bent to get those standards pushed down to the preschool years so that we can set expectations for young children.

Much of that discourse is probably well intentioned, and it's really about making learning opportunities more productive in some way. But much of it is very one-sided, and it doesn't take account—as we would as parents, as people, as teachers—of the need to affirm children and who they are, to support them in a way that doesn't continually say to them: "You're less than. You're more than. You're better than. You're worse than. You measure up. You don't measure up." And to speak in those other terms in the discourse today is to be dismissed, quite often, as soft and gushy.

Don Ernst: As I was just recently dismissed.

LDH: Yes. And one can become cowed in the discourse. One can say, as John was suggesting we ought no longer say, "Well, we'll just have to adjust to the new 'this' or the new 'that.'" I think it's important now for a very articulate voice to continue to be raised on behalf of the human side of our lives together and on behalf of our children.

Those of us who work directly with kids see and feel their experiences and their pain and their emotions and their relationships with one another, with us, and with the society as a whole in a much more tangible way than do people who sit far away from that reality and make pronouncements about what will be done to kids in schools. Rarely, in the standards conversation, are adults talking about heightening the standards for *themselves*, making themselves more responsible for the quality of experiences they provide in schools, for the quality of policies they enact. They're talking about laying it all on the kids and saying, "Let's hold them accountable. Forget about us." I think we've got to speak to that omission.

JG: Don, in regard to the standards they're talking about now and this school-to-work relationship, were these people talking about academic standards?

Don Ernst: Both, actually, and about the melding of the academic standards and the school-to-work stuff.

LDH: Creating certifications that will tell people whether they can graduate and, what's more, whether they can get a job.

Don Ernst: Right.

JG: I want to go back to something that Roger said. If I heard him correctly, he was saying that if a certain group of people know what it is they're doing, he would be more worried than if they were unwitting. I thought that you said that, but if you didn't, I'll assume you did *[Laughter.]* . . . for rhetorical purposes. There's a book that's beginning to gather attention, the David C. Berliner and Bruce J. Biddle book, *The Manufactured Crisis*, and it is tipping the scales quite the other way.[4] In effect, using my own language, the authors are saying, "They done a job on us." That is, "they" created a crisis in schooling around the wrong issues. Berliner and Biddle also suggest that this is virtually a conspiracy. I don't personally accept the conspiracy theme, but it looks as though there are a lot of people in the country who promote a certain way of classifying people. Our schools have been doing this: the sorting process. Now we seem to be moving into the work domain to do that. And if you look back about a hundred and sixty years or so to the Working Man's Party, which flourished in major cities like Philadelphia and Boston, you will notice that the party platforms sharply distinguished between education and schooling on the one hand and the right to work on the other.

I wrote a piece a few years back called "Beyond Half an Education,"[5] in which I expressed deep concern about the degree to which society is lowering the value of the skills we need to sustain the infrastructure and tying these in with academic standards that would cut out of the workplace most of the people our family depends upon. One of our neighbors said to us not long ago that he got great criticism from other neighbors because he chose to paint his own house. That sort of lowered the status of the neighborhood: as though what you do is hire a painter; you don't paint your own house. This undervaluing of these skills in their own right and setting academic prerequisites for them fits into this scheme of sorting and classifying, and it makes it difficult for some people to enter into the workforce and be able to, because of income, enjoy choice.

I see Mary Ellen Finch beginning to stir back there, and so I'll give you the microphone, Mary Ellen.

Mary Ellen Finch: Mary Ellen Finch, St. Louis Consortium for Educational Renewal. My question really is directed to Ted, but I hope to hear from others. I was encouraged and intrigued by Ted's comment about what he sees as a grassroots movement in support of children. I haven't seen that particular movement in Missouri. Missouri has to be shown, obviously. *[Laughter.]* My question is two-part. I want to know more about what Ted's talking about: how this particular movement interfaces, or doesn't interface, with the movement that I do see in Missouri and around the country, when people are coming in and we're having many, many mass meetings in the St. Louis area. And in my hands yesterday was put a paper that said if your school mentions Sizer, if your school mentions outcomes, if your school mentions Goodlad, if your school mentions a whole raft of things, then call this number. Is there an organized movement against school reform? That's question number one.

Question number two goes back to the grassroots. In terms of equity, who are the grassroots? Are they well-educated parents who are pushing for certain things, or is it a really egalitarian, grassroots movement? So, Ted, I want to hear more from you.

TS: I'd like to know what that phone number is. *[Laughter.]*

I think the deliberate organization by certain so-called right-wing groups for local political activity is a terrific thing. The essence of American democracy is local. All politics is local, all education is local. And what we should not do is curse the attack—those of us who happen to disagree with it—but to make sure that other voices are heard, that people who have a different belief about democratic education gather the necessary local and state political clout. And this is happening. More than a few schools in the Coalition of Essential Schools have been targets, and most, I'm happy to say, have overcome. They've overcome because parents and teachers and local political leaders have examined the issues, have linked arms, have organized, have put candidates forward, and have made sure that folks went to the polls. So, to me, the organized and resurgent interest at the local level spearheaded by certain groups, many of which don't admire what I and my colleagues stand for in public education, is a plus.

My reading of some of this, and also my reading of the kind of meeting that Don Ernst went to, is a little different. I was struck at the annual meeting of the Education Commission of the States this last summer by the difference in the body language of the state political leaders in public and in private. Publicly, they exuded assurance, policy, and an attitude of "We've got to do this"; but in private they were scared out of their minds. There was a tentativeness on the part of governors and governors' staffs privately, which was utterly nonpartisan and which reinforced my hunch that what we have out there, more than anything, is confusion. Folks don't know what to do. And when you don't know what you want to do—what you should do—you cleave to the familiar. The familiar is to go back to the old Progressive strategy of getting a system solution. The worst of the standard-setting movement may be the death rattle of Progressivism, by which people of goodwill get together and figure out how to solve a problem and create a scientific—not political—way of dealing with it. And while I think there are enormous benefits in the so-called standards movement—it's raised all sorts of good issues—this notion of reducing it to tests and certificates and who can go forward and who can go back smacks more of the early twentieth century than it does of the late twentieth century. So, I think what you're describing and what Don is describing are examples of the useful confrontations going on, the swirling around, the confusion which presents, as I say, a great deal of opportunity as well as fear.

Now, where are the grassroots movements? They're driven by teachers and parents. They're driven largely, so far, in communities serving the poor and the nonwhite. They are driven by people who have local experience, and as we've seen in a few parts of the country—again, notably in this city—when those schools link arms and when they are organized in the best sense, when one of them is attacked in some irresponsible way, the others respond with them. They're politically savvy and, in effect, they're operating increasingly as school districts. They are political entities. I take heart from the willingness of people who know the realities because they live with them saying, "Just going along or coping in the short range is not enough; we're getting creamed by only dealing with the short range."

I don't think I'm living in a fool's paradise to think that the kind of momentum behind grassroots, local-level reform might rapidly accelerate simply because there's so much confusion out there.

JG: Anyone else on the panel want to comment? . . . Susan, okay.

Susan Roper: Hi. I'm Susan Roper, and my name tag says California, so I guess I'm representing about thirty-two million people. *[Laughter.]* I wanted to allude to an article that David Elkind wrote that appeared in the *Kappan* a couple of issues back.[6] He describes a very different kind of family than the safe haven, Gary, that I heard you describing. He says that today's family is more like a busy train station, and that people take breaks at home from their busy schedules. Often these breaks are taken by solitary individuals: the family meal has become less and less common.

As I pondered that image, a couple of things occurred to me. One was that the safe haven brings up a lot of nostalgia, I think, for those of us who were raised in a safe haven. But I wonder if that wasn't purchased at a pretty big price in terms of the person who generally kept that safe haven together, usually the mother. That role has changed, and so we have the busy train station. Given those very different kinds of images, would you comment, Gary, and perhaps others, as to whether or not this new kind of family as the busy train station is equally able to prepare children for living in a democracy, or better, or worse?

Just one other quick point that David Elkind makes: he says that we have images that we need to have to keep functioning. One of our images of our children is that they're very independent and very capable, and he uses the movie *Home Alone* as the metaphor for what we want to think about our children because we need to think that. We're not there at home in the safe haven taking care of our children so, by God, they'd better be able to take care of themselves. I'd be interested in your comments on that different image.

GF: The first thing I want to say is: "I don't know." This is a real crystal-ball kind of problem. I think what we do know is that we're in the midst of a massive transformation in this notion of primary and secondary associations, in how the family and the public are built and created. The only things that seem evident to me at this point are that the things we think are the requisite features of a civil government or a civil state or civitas, a public, are formed in family life, in the way we rear our children; that part of why we see this disintegration of public life is because we're seeing this disintegration of private life; that the kinds of private lives that we're leading now, the kinds of primary associations that we have, aren't sustaining the kind of public that we think we need; and that we're reaping the result of a rather despairing, very poor private life or set of primary associations. What's all the more remarkable is that our public policy isn't addressing it. It's so evident, I think to many of us, that something is wrong here, and it's also evident that so much policy is simply, as Don Ernst was saying, ignoring it. I agree with Elkind's conception in many ways, but it also seems to me extraordinarily dangerous and debilitating.

LDH: I left a "train station" home this morning, shoving bagels into my kids' mouths and forgetting to grab one for myself on the way here. It's clear that it makes a difference in lots of ways that have positives and negatives for raising kids for a democratic life with egalitarian images and values. But whether one is talking about that kind of a train station starting point for kids when they leave the house in the morning and go to school, or other settings which are severely stressed and challenged—the half a million kids who are homeless, the one out of five who live in poverty, and on and on and on—I think an implication of this set of changes is that schools must become more communitarian as families and communities become less able, for a variety of reasons, to give children intensive, sustained attention and support. For me, this is one of the key reasons why the one hundred small, new high schools in New York City that are replacing the big warehouse environments that were so dehumanizing and impersonal are really important as images of twenty-first century democratic schools. People who, from the grassroots, are creating places where kids can be known, can be part of a community, can be cared for, can stay in groups with the same teacher for longer stretches of time, where someone really looks after them in some sense, are absolutely essential to deal with this transition, whether one thinks it's good, bad, or indifferent, and whatever the causes or sources of it. We can't both sustain the transformations in families and communities and maintain these impersonal settings where kids are just numbers, and hope that at the other end of it students emerge with really serious kinds of learning and with the ability to care for themselves and to relate to others.

JG: Donna, you were wanting to get into this.

DK: We're talking about human relationships, and it's not soft and touchy-feely; there are hard data to back this up. We need redundancy of adults who are self-responsible and responsive hanging out with kids, whether we do that by making smaller school contexts, community centers, youth groups—there's a host of ways, and we probably ought to do them in a host of ways. This is one of those cases where we ought to waste some money on children. And there are a lot of studies if we're looking for hard data on what difference this makes in the society, in the lives of kids. The Werner study in Kauai, a thirty-year longitudinal study, presents as one of its main conclusions that those kids who had some adult who would hang out with them and be responsive to them were the young people who became very responsible, participating members in the community.[7] This isn't just something we imagine; there are data there to show that, and certainly this would be one case where I think we ought to read Benjamin Barber and say, "It's time to waste something on the kids."

JG: Which introduces Benjamin Barber again.

BB: Obviously there's a circle between public and private institutions, between primary institutions like the family and schools. We need good family life to support students who want to come to the schools so they can learn, and we need good schools to reinforce and support those values, so that the kids who both go home to their families and eventually create families, create the kinds of families that contribute to a democratic society.

I think there are two things that need to be said. One is the question of where as educators we can best put our resources. If we were at a social work convention, maybe it would be appropriate to be talking about how social work can, in a sense, get at families. But we're teachers, we're educators, and although it may be that we should leave our schools and universities and primary schools and go into the home and try to deal with parents, and so on, I suspect that we wouldn't do a very good job at that. So in terms of *our* levers of power, such as they are—they may not be very effectual, but they're the only ones we have as educators—it seems to me that we have to talk about how we can make schools more responsive to that situation and make schools educators of liberty for young people.

The second thing I want to say, though, is that the circumstances to which we look when we talk about the decline of the family are not accidental or historical or simply the consequence of inevitable forces over which nobody has much control. We constructed the social world in which we're now living and about which we now complain a lot. There are two kinds of dysfunctional families; I think we need to be very clear about that. One kind is the kind that Linda talked about: it's the stressed family, the family where children are born to poverty, where parents are on crack, where there's maybe only one parent, trying very hard both to make a living and to take care of kids. Such families are deeply stressed, and we know how inadequate, despite the goodwill of parents, they often are. But there's another kind of family, the railroad station family, which is a construction of the marketplace and a construction of some other social choices, some of which are very beneficial: equality between men and women, and so on. If women are going to become just as successful as men, then nobody is much left to deal with the kids anymore. We get the railroad station homes. And that's the result of choices that do have real benefits to the society, but they also have costs. We've created that part of the world as a consequence of, on the one hand, inequality, racism, and the maldistribution of wealth, and on the other hand, as a result of a marketplace society in which we're all trying to make it big and be successful in the world's terms.

And it's our children who are getting—excuse the expression—deeply screwed by both forms of social construction. The inequality and the fast track—the slow track and the fast track—both exist at the expense of our children. Then, of course, people turn to our schools and to us and say, "Fix it.

Make it better." And then we begin to say, "Well, we can't just fix things through the schools, we somehow have to get back to the families, get back to the marketplace." But we don't know how to do that so we're caught up in a very difficult cycle where the levers of power left to us are probably inadequate to deal with the situation because of other choices that the society at large has made.

Until we come back to the central question of who we want to pay the costs of our choices about distribution of wealth, and our choices about career tracks and professionalism and how we make money in our society, I think again and again it's our children who are going to pay the price. And we will always be in the difficult position of trying to fiddle with relatively ineffectual levers of power in the educational realm and constantly trying to look beyond the schools, as Gary does, and say, "Well, how can we get beyond the schools?" And, of course, we really can't—as educators. Maybe as citizens we can; maybe as people who are part of the political marketplace that creates these choices we can. But I think we don't want to pretend that the issues we face that disable us as educators—broken families, train station families—are just the result of some vague historical forces. We made that world. Now we're having a very hard time living in it, and a lot of Americans don't want to look at the way in which we made the world and the values in terms of which that world was constructed.

RS: Maybe, Benjamin, we can go into the homes a little bit in terms of, say, what I saw at an elementary school in El Paso several weeks ago. At one time, many of the parents were discouraged from even coming into the school; they had to wait for their children outside. What happened, through a very good principal and some work by people with the Industrial Areas Foundation and Texas Interfaith Organization, Ernesto Cortes and Sister Maribeth Larkin, and the hiring of a community organizer (a parent educator, in effect) is remarkable. I listened to a number of parents who told us that several years ago they wouldn't have even dreamed that they would be sitting before us as a panel talking to us about what they were doing. One mother told us that she had learned about power and about community. They had also learned about the distinction between parent *involvement*—that is, where parents come in and pop popcorn on Fridays and make the copies and do all those sorts of things—and parent *engagement*—where their children could see that parents were in the classroom as partners, not just running around and doing the gofer errands here and there, but they were actually empowered. And this was a conscious, educative process of going out into the community to individual parents' homes and telling them that they wanted them at the school. The school had hired somebody specifically to do that recruiting.

So I think there are some practical ways in which you can actually teach people about their powers and their rights and responsibilities, not only for that school, but for other things: those same parents turned around and leaned on the city council down there at El Paso because there's a very dangerous crosswalk. Kids have been injured. And when the superintendent called up the principal and screamed, "Can't you control your parents?" she responded with, "Well, no." *[Laughter.]* And so I think there are some ways that we can start moving on some of these things.

Mark O'Shea: Mark O'Shea from Metropolitan State College of Denver. I'm thinking about the role of teachers in all of this. Dr. Goodlad, following your remarks in Wyoming not long ago, I decided to take the chance myself and talk about the moral dimensions of teaching to elementary teachers at a breakfast in an urban school in Denver. I did so with some trepidation; you had the advantage of your renown and scholarship, and I would say, to a large extent, an attentive and receptive audience in Wyoming. I was speaking to teachers who knew me only casually, and probably didn't really know where I was coming from at all. And as I spoke to them about these notions of abiding principles that teachers should have and their role to help children move along in responsible decision making, ultimately for their own participation in society, they were receptive. They were very receptive, indeed. But at the same time, they were timid. I was concerned for them because they approached me with such thoughts as: "Of course, we won't teach morals here. We have a community that's afraid about teaching morals—that we would come in and profess our own morals to the children." Further, to a large extent, they felt that they would be hard-pressed to defend their role as having a moral element attached to their predominant role of imparting knowledge and skills.

Could you, perhaps, as a panel, respond to the notion of how teachers might work within the present context of schooling, putting aside notions of how we might reform the institution or change the organization, but deal with schools the way they are now and help teachers assume that role more fully? Because I really came away with the sense that they wanted to.

JG: Let me begin with a comment and then there will be a couple of others. There's one caution that John White has made in his fairly recent book, *Education and the Good Life*.[8] He warns about this word "moral." We use it in our work all the time, and as you say, to a receptive audience. But even then, with our book, *The Moral Dimensions of Teaching*,[9] we've had people who, on one hand, say, "Oh, isn't this wonderful? At last people are going to worry about alcohol, drugs, and sex. That's what these people are against." So we get that. And then on the other hand, people ask, "Whose morals are going to be taught?" What White says is: Look, why don't we deal with the cultivation of dispositions? Dispositions that are caring, dispositions that have elements of justice, dispositions on which I think everyone would agree. In fact, if one goes back to the roots of all the world's great religions, one will find these dispositions. If one goes to the end products of rational thinkers, again you end up with the same dispositions. So I think the first thing I would say is that probably in most settings, particularly the individual school setting, we need to talk about the cultivation of dispositions in regard to how we treat one another. That will take us away, I think, from this "we can't teach morals" business. I think this is a good caution on White's part that others may want to comment on. He *[Mark O'Shea]* had a broader question—

BB: The complaint of the Right is that what you call "dispositions" is what they call "secular humanism," which is a series of platitudes about niceness and reciprocity and tolerance that don't add up to any real particular kinds of behavior in which they're interested. I don't think it's so easy to gloss it by assuming that if we somehow soften the language of morals and turn it into dispositions, in terms of being nice to one another, somehow we can get away from the tough issues that people who really want to teach morals want to teach. Because it's their complaint precisely that the dispositional approach, as it were, is what has undermined the ability of young people to really, say, understand that abortion is murder—if that's what you think—or that choice is an absolute right of women over their own reproductive facilities and so forth.

That's why I'm not sure we ought to be engaged in the teaching of morals; that's the one thing I think the school can't do. I think what it can do is teach young people something about how to live with people who have fundamentally different moral dispositions and values and nonetheless with whom they have to live. People who think choice is murder and people who think the abortion lobby is only interested in something that women themselves and feminists should be interested in: those two sets of people nonetheless have to live together without shooting one another down in the streets. How do we do that? Those dispositions, which are democratic dispositions, if you like, it seems to me, can be taught. But the minute you get into saying we're really going to teach morals, what people do mean by that is teach that abortion is wrong; teach that Christ is our savior; or that, if you're Jewish, that Christ is *not* our savior. But it's not like there's a disposition in which one or the other of those two things are true, or you can hold both at the same time. And I think the moral Right in America has a very clear view of what it means by morality, and the rest of us try to talk about dispositions, hoping that will make it go away. And it won't go away.

Steven Baugh: Steven Baugh, Superintendent, Alpine School District in Utah, and a part of the BYU–Public School Partnership. The strength of the Coalition of Essential Schools to me is that it's based on a set of principles, superb principles. The strength of the National Network, I believe, is that it's based on fundamentally sound principles. My concern is that although we are moving in a positive direction—perhaps arithmetically, in some ways maybe even geometrically—the problems are moving exponentially. To the point: are you impatient or discouraged with the growth of these movements? And I don't mean to make them sound prescriptive, because again I think it's the principles that are the most important part of it, but there are only sixteen sites and twenty-five universities and three hundred partner schools in the NNER and perhaps several hundred Essential Schools, and we have fifteen thousand school districts and problems moving exponentially. Speak to that: the growth of the movement. Are we getting to some kind of critical mass that we can really make a difference? I hope we are. I'm not sure that we are. Would you please comment?

TS: I'm dismayed at how difficult it is to carry out common sense in many cases: common sense in schools. And I am dismayed but not surprised by the enormous momentum of tradition. That's the down side. The up side is that the number of schools involved is now about 920 in the Coalition. There are also many schools that are, in fact, kin. I don't know the number of schools that are influenced by what my colleagues are doing in schools around the country, but I have the sense that it's far more than it was five years ago. And so the hope is that the ideas and the bearing witness on the part of schools that have been able to break through and increasingly have kids who are different for it, that that will resonate. So, while I'm distressed at how difficult it is, I feel that it is ever easier as the record gets out.

JG: Responding for the Network, two things. First of all, Roger has pointed out in his chapter in his book, *Democracy, Education, and the Schools*,[10] that some 75 percent of a future teacher's postsecondary education comes through the arts and sciences. So it is rather dismaying to find in some of our settings people still saying: "Why do the arts and sciences need to be involved in the renewal of teacher education?" I think it's just common sense that they do. There's a big chunk of it, and what we're talking about here, on this panel, is more likely to be done—or the appropriate place to begin it is—in the education young people are getting in the arts and sciences part of their higher education programs. Then there's a special job to be done in regard to what this means in the context, Mark, of the people you were speaking with the other day.

Let me say one more thing, and it goes largely to Mary Ellen Finch's initial point, and that is, in talking about what's going on in the schools, the degree to which the schools are penetrating the university and the university is penetrating the schools is very positive. This afternoon I will go over to Montclair State University and their surrounding school districts where we will celebrate the founding of the first center of pedagogy, something that John Dewey recommended in 1903, and I picked up many years later. So we are at least creating the conditions for the conversation that needs to go on among these groups.

The thing that discourages us, Steve, or the criticism we get, is that we're very small. Even though we include sixteen settings, twenty-five colleges and universities, nearly a hundred school districts, and three hundred partner schools, we are very small, but nonetheless probably one of the largest educational initiatives in the country and the only one that is deliberately focusing on the renewal of both schooling and teacher education. The purpose of this symposium this morning is to enlarge the conversation. So, Mark, when you talk about your dealing with those teachers where you are, right in Denver, this is the kind of thing we would hope to happen. Where we are right now is to say, "Look, we can't expand this National Network at the level, the intensity at which we work at it now, very much. We have to stay under twenty settings or so, given our resources and our energies. But we can expand the conversation." And this symposium is intended to do that, to alert as many people as possible to the issues we are discussing here this morning: how important they are, and the degree to which we can participate at a whole array of levels in this discussion. For that penetration, Steve, we need to look at how all of the settings can expand the conversation, then how we in the Network can expand the conversation. And that's part of what we're about.

I'm very much with Ted. I'm finding the same thing he is finding: that these ideas are resonating. Tradition, the way we've always done it, bogs us down terribly, and there's an intensive effort involved to change all that. Ted and I met in San Francisco about eight or ten years ago, I recall, both terribly exhausted. His book *Horace's Compromise*[11] had just come out, and he was going across the country because of demand. Likewise, my book *A Place Called School*[12] had just come out, and I was going across the country because of demand. I would say we were both very depressed. Five years later we were still depressed. *[Laughter.]* Five years after *that,* we're both saying we're up, we're encouraged, we're hopeful, even in the face of the kinds of things we're talking about this morning.

And so the message to the Coalition folks, to the National Network folks, and to others is: try to expand this conversation. Penetrate further in regard to the incredible importance of education to democracy, the need for democracy to be safe for education, and from that, whether or not we can have a public education system that will do the job.

I think that at this stage we should break it up. I want to thank the members of the panel again for the superb way in which they entered into this: getting papers to me on time, getting here, participating as they did. And thank you for being a great audience. *[Applause.]*

Notes

1. Benjamin R. Barber, "America Skips School: Why We Talk So Much about Education and Do So Little," *Harper's Magazine* 287 (November 1993): 39–46; and "Searching for Civil Society," *National Civic Review* 84 (Spring 1995): 114–18.
2. Gary D Fenstermacher, "The Absence of Democratic and Educational Ideals from Contemporary Educational Reform Initiatives," *Educational Horizons* 73 (Winter 1995): 70–80.
3. Benjamin R. Barber, *An Aristocracy of Everyone: The Politics of Education and the Future of America* (New York: Ballantine Books, 1992).
4. David C. Berliner and Bruce J. Biddle, *The Manufactured Crisis: Myths, Fraud, and the Attack on America's Public Schools* (Reading, Mass.: Addison-Wesley, 1995).
5. John I. Goodlad, "Beyond Half an Education," *Education Week*, 19 February 1992, pp. 44, 34.
6. David Elkind, "School and Family in the Postmodern World," *Phi Delta Kappan* 77 (September 1995): 8–14.
7. Emmy E. Werner and Ruth S. Smith, *Overcoming the Odds: High Risk Children from Birth to Adulthood* (Ithaca, N.Y.: Cornell University Press, 1992).
8. John White, *Education and the Good Life: Autonomy, Altruism, and the National Curriculum* (New York: Teachers College Press, Columbia University, 1991).
9. John I. Goodlad, Roger Soder, and Kenneth A. Sirotnik, eds., *The Moral Dimensions of Teaching* (San Francisco: Jossey-Bass, 1990).
10. Roger Soder, "Teaching the Teachers of the People," in *Democracy, Education, and the Schools*, ed. Roger Soder (San Francisco: Jossey-Bass, 1996), pp. 244–74.
11. Theodore R. Sizer, *Horace's Compromise: The Dilemma of the American High School* (Boston: Houghton Mifflin, 1984).
12. John I. Goodlad, *A Place Called School: Prospects for the Future* (New York: McGraw-Hill, 1984).

Part Three

A *Public Agenda*?

Chapter Nine

Reprise and a Look Ahead

John I. Goodlad

The introduction to this volume outlined and placed in historical perspective some of the major concepts addressed both in the papers that became the chapters of this book and in the conversations that followed. I revisit several of these in this chapter. In so doing, I present views that align with those of my colleagues but for which I take full responsibility.

Some Concepts Revisited

Education is an adventure of the self. It is natural, then, to think of education as a matter of private purpose and experience. However, adventures of the self are experienced in public contexts. The self is shaped through interpretation of social encounters; the nature of these encounters is critically important. The private purposes of education—the cultivation and satisfaction of the self—can be pursued only in the company of public purpose. How we are with others has a great deal to do with how we are with ourselves.

Schooling, on the other hand, is a sociopolitical invention that seeks to design a context or contexts for shaping many "selfs" toward predetermined ends. Schools reflect the dominant ideology or several competing ideologies regarding what these ends should be and what should be embedded in their practices to attain them. Children can and do become educated and acquire personal identity as selfs without schools. The central idea driving schools is that part of this educating should be guided and conducted to advance not just the maturation of the self but also some public need or good. The definitions of public need and good and the prevailing balance in the satisfaction of both private and public interest vary widely from society to society.

There are in societies—even authoritarian ones—beliefs best described as moral imperatives that transfer education from willy-nilly adventures along miscellaneous, often uncharted, pathways to processes that guide these adventures through contingencies arranged in the environment. These contingencies, in turn, align with dominant belief systems of each culture or society. They range from mandated spheres of human freedom with punishment built into the boundary lines much as cattle are contained by electrified fences, to laws that specify what may and may not be done in a wide range of situations, to principles of conduct that assume human beings to be thinking creatures capable of understanding that personal well-being requires a civil society. This last mode requires the most from the educational infrastructure, part of which is schooling that balances private and public purpose.

Democracy is the descriptive word most often and consistently applied to humankind's many attempts to define and provide some ideal balance between individual and collective freedom and individual and collective responsibility. And the example most often cited over the past century to illustrate both democracy's promise and its daunting nature is "the American democracy." Unfortunately, disproportionate attention has been given, both externally and within the United States, to issues of democratic governance rather than to the symbiotics of civil relationships. Within this dominant emphasis, in turn, deviations from patriotic symbolism have stimulated more rhetorical outrage than has the plight of the poor and suffering. For a society to rest its case for the virtues of democracy on mechanisms of governance alone, however nobly framed, is to place both that society and democracy itself at risk.

It is by no means an exaggeration to say, "As goes a nation's educational infrastructure, so goes its democracy." Nor is it an overstatement to say, "As goes its democracy, so goes a nation's educational infrastructure." The two are inextricably entwined and sensitively interdependent.

Contextual contingencies would serve only as gentle reminders of public responsibilities if humans began their existence with civil dispositions already full-blown. They would love themselves, one another, and their world. But, for better or for worse, each person begins anew a process of self-transcendence that, for some, advances little beyond narcissism. Unfortunately, parenthood does not automatically bring with it the wisdom required for enculturating the young in civil dispositions. Consequently, an infrastructure that includes laws must make safe but not restrictive an educative context that balances individual freedom and civic responsibility. The creation, development, and refinement of this infrastructure is by far the most challenging of all enterprises.

Recurring Themes

Asked to select the overarching theme in the foregoing chapters and conversations, I would offer the following: We must take care of one another. My colleagues argue not for greater attention to salvation of the individual soul—that domain is already quite cluttered with diverse and often conflicting prognostications—but for greater attention to the moral civil arts: from those of how we behave in private to those of how we are with one another to those of the common good. A central issue is whether the process of self-transcendence involves primarily or even exclusively an extension of the individual moral arts or whether new learnings characterize acquisition of the moral arts of community ties and of the common good.

The major subtheme is the tension between private purpose and the common good and how this tension enters into public understanding of what education is and what schools are for. Unless our young people are educated in a context today of virtually passionate caring about the ecosystem—social, political, and natural—that sustains them, the heritage they leave their children will be meager. Unless their education helps them to sift carefully out of the past what is most sustaining for today, their search for moral compasses to guide one choice of direction over another will be erratic and daunting.

The social and political context is that of democracy—specifically that of the United States of America. The connection between democracy, education, and the conduct of our schools was close to the surface in both the chapters of Part One and the conversations of Part Two. There was agreement on a public purpose for education and schooling that sustains both civility and civitas (a body of people constituting a politically organized community). A democracy depends on an educative infrastructure that teaches appreciation for both liberty and the responsibilities that go with nurturing freedom. For that infrastructure to be robust, in turn, there must be widespread belief in and practice of the civil moral arts that mark mature social and political democracies. The concluding chapter in Part One raises the question of the current status of the necessary belief and the degree of passion regarding its support.

Michael Oakeshott wrote that conversation intended to bring out alternatives and possibilities regarding issues such as the ones discussed here "is impossible in the absence of a diversity of voices."[1] The contributors to this little volume were picked with such diversity in mind. Other voices found their way into our conversations. Had Mary Catherine Bateson been with us in person, our references to *all* people would have become even more explicit and it would have been necessary for me to expand the overarching concept: We must take care of our habitat and one another here on this earth.[2] We must be carefully taught to understand that the species that destroys its habitat destroys itself.[3] Had Jane Roland Martin been with us, we would have heard more about how education directed not only toward preservation of our habitat but also toward preservation of our cultural wealth might contribute to cultivation of the moral civil arts: Cultural wealth "encompasses the institutions and practices, rites and rituals, beliefs and skills, attitudes and values, and world views and localized modes of thinking and acting of all members of society over the whole range of contexts."[4] When those with relevant views are not at the table, their written thoughts are a readily available resource.

For those who were at the table, there appears to have been an implicit context that brought an urgency to their voices: awareness of widespread angst. It is an angst that eludes definition even as elements of it are widely displayed on televised talk shows and between the covers of books and magazines. On the surface, it appears to be an angst of the human spirit brought on by perceived disparities between inflated expectations and deflated realities—a kind of national midlife crisis. The observation of Alexis de Tocqueville a century and a half ago appears to have at least some relevance today: "It is odd to watch with what feverish ardor the Americans pursue prosperity and how they are ever tormented by the shadowy suspicion that they may not have chosen the shortest route to get it."[5] It is interesting to note the frequency with which pundits refer to Tocqueville in seeking descriptors and even analyses of current angst. It is interesting to note also the parallel between Tocqueville's "souls seem suddenly to break the restraining bonds of matter and rush impetuously heavenward"[6] and the extent of today's search for solace in the divine.

Tocqueville saw this "enthusiastic, almost fierce spirituality"[7] as driven by the compelling needs of the soul. Seymour Sarason views the roots of today's "rush to God" quite differently. He argues that belief in a divinity and a sense of belonging to a "geographically circumscribed human community"[8] were once closely joined. But in modern times these beliefs were severed through the impoverishment of the ties that bind one to a human community. Having lost a psychological sense of community, many people have become obsessed with spirituality. Education and schools can do much for the community moral arts but little for the faith that must guide the search for salvation of the individual human soul. Hence, preservation and sustenance of democracy requires that the public purpose of the former function not be overrun by the private purpose of the latter quest.

There is more to prevailing angst, however, than the psychological sense of loss that comes from severance of community ties. Had those of us who participated in the conversation recorded on preceding pages been privileged to listen in on the conversation that lay behind the papers published in the Winter 1996 issue of *Daedalus*, our conversation might have turned more to the little-talked-about role of education and schooling in the alleviation of little-talked-about "social suffering." Is there, even among those privileged enough not to experience social suffering personally, enough awareness of social suffering generally to engender angst? There, but for the grace of God, go I?

There are two sides to the impact of awareness of social suffering, even when not directly experienced. One is empathy accompanied by feelings of helplessness; the other is alarm accompanied by selfishness. In his preface to the issue of *Daedalus* referred to above, editor Stephen Graubard refers to a chaotic and cruel twentieth century.[9] He writes,

> There is only scant appreciation of the conditions that exist in the world today where the experiences of different peoples have been so diverse, where so many harbor memories of dangers barely averted, of families destroyed, disasters brought on not by personal fault or negligence but by the accident of birth. Theories of collective guilt, that made whole communities the legitimate target of cruel and life-threatening punishment, that led millions of ordinary men and women to suffer humiliation, injury, or death, are integral parts of a historical tale that has different emphases, and is differently interpreted, in various corners of the globe.[10]

We catch glimpses of these brutalities on the televised news; we are horrified and empathetic. They are what the promises of an earlier enlightened age depicted as soon to be eliminated by modern science and technology. That innocence has been largely lost. The technologies of today rarely address the moral dilemmas of social suffering around the world while we are again told that modern science and technology will remove their source. Thus assured, we are advised to turn to more uplifting matters here at home, such as celebrations of the American democracy and of being the most powerful nation on earth.

There is little in history, however—even history spanning just a few generations—to suggest that a nation's power and the contentment of its people go hand in hand. Feelings of pride have only passing impact on the vicissitudes of daily life. National celebrations, even of the ascent of liberty in a democratic society, do not dispel individual and collective angst. Nor do these celebrations put an end to all that fosters this angst—and there appears to be much that does, including the messages of the technological medium that is to usher in a more splendid era. Glimpses of social suffering abroad may create temporary empathy; glimpses of social suffering close up create fear. Will the joblessness around me be my lot? How is the turbulence over health insurance to affect me? Will advancing age find me a prisoner in an abode surrounded by violence? Or worse? One who does not personally experience social suffering often anticipates it. Such thoughts are powerful producers of angst.

One must be a powerfully committed believer in education to advance in this context its healing properties. But it was on such a note of hope that our participants concluded their conversation. The essays in *Daedalus* suggest the depth and breadth of the educational effort required: from cross-disciplinary inquiry into the contemporary world designed to bring new understandings of nature and human nature to the table, to the development of educative communities that are safe for the teachings required. To place this educational burden on schools alone is folly:

> Humanizing the level at which interventions are organized means focusing planning and evaluation on the interpersonal space of suffering, the local, ethnographic context of action. . . . Policy-making

> from the ground up can only succeed, however, if these local worlds are more effectively projected into national and international discourses on human problems. . . . How to reframe the language of policies and programs so that large-scale social forces are made to relate to biography and local history will require interdisciplinary engagements that bring alternative perspectives from the humanities, the social sciences, and the health sciences to bear on human problems. The goal is to reconstruct the object of inquiry and the purposes of practice.[11]

Schooling, Education, and Public Policy

The implications for the purposes and practices of education and schooling in our time are enormous. As the authors of the passage quoted in the previous paragraph point out: "The starting point of policymakers and program builders needs to be the understanding that they can . . . do harm."[12] Today's policymakers, at both state and federal levels, have been slow to read the danger signs along the paths of school reform that dominated their rhetoric, policies, and interventions during the first years of the concluding decade of the twentieth century.

Two egregious errors stand out. First, policymakers elevated the role of schools in individual and national well-being to an unrealistic level. Second, by fastening on school reform as the road to this well-being, they confused the later failure of reform with the failure of schooling itself. The fallout from this haplessness was widespread disillusionment with public schooling that in no way matched the performance of schools in regard to their traditional function. The response of the media to a poll taken in the late 1980s and repeated in the mid-1990s should have elicited more than silence from our politicians. In the first, the selection of Japan as the leading economic power by those polled added fuel to the pyre of school criticism enthusiastically fanned by the media. In the second, the selection of the United States as the foremost economic power was relegated to the back pages and off the screen of politicians. Little wonder that David Berliner and Bruce Biddle were quick to title their analysis of these "school reform" years *The Manufactured Crisis*.[13] Given the connection between inflated expectations and perceived deflated realities, it is realistic to believe that ill-guided, politically driven school reform contributed to individual and collective angst.

The first error might be attributed to unwitting policymakers believing that the American people could be aroused to interest in education only through exhorting the instrumental role of the schools in creating jobs—an attribution that would disparage politicians' views of their constituents and cast a bad light on the priorities of the American people. But it is much more difficult to find a pony in the manure pile when examining the second error. It can be put down primarily to political motivations, tinged with the monetary considerations that so commonly accompany them: During the concluding decade of the century, two of the most popular ideas condoned or championed by policymakers were the privatization of schooling and the matching of schools with parents' interests (and hence placing private over public purpose in the function of schools). The words of Jesus Christ regarding his executioners come to mind: They knoweth not what they do. Of course, the lasting influence of Jesus stems in large part from his undiluted, unwavering charity of spirit. Lacking this maturity of charitable thought, I am more inclined to believe that they knoweth what they did, but they knoweth wrong.

My colleagues in the conversation recorded here have already well stated the connection between education and the individual, community, and humankind moral arts that make it possible for us to care for one another—everyone—and our habitat, and to alleviate the human suffering that will always characterize the course of our future. They have well stated the critical public purpose of public schooling in the cultivation of these arts. They have stressed the need for our schools to be *commonly good*. And they have stressed the necessity of widely extending to our people the choices of schools now enjoyed only by the affluent (choices that eliminate for many of the affluent the need to pay more for the choice of a private school). They have exhorted the need for a community infrastructure designed to support healthy self-transcendence for everyone and the mitigation of suffering and its sources. Such an infrastructure is educative; a robust system of public schooling is at its heart.

Surely in these agreements there is a policy agenda worthy of attention and policymakers worthy of its advancement. Rhetoric long on the common good and short on the promise of personal aggrandizement would be a good beginning. But, wait, there is a third error that must be addressed.

Early in 1996, there was still another education summit—this one of governors, corporate executives, and a scattering of educators, mostly from governmental and professional organizations. The theme was that of its political time: standards—more of them, more clearly defined, and higher. Left by themselves, such standards will do no harm; indeed, some good will trickle down. Exhorted and clothed in high expectations, with no more provision for the conditions required for their attainment than their omission at the summit portends, and still more disillusionment with our schools—and hence more angst—will be engendered.

One passing reference to conditions—by the president of the United States—dampens one's spirits somewhat regarding prospects for the end of folly in school reform. He expressed admiration for the example of private, entrepreneurial enterprise represented in a highly publicized initiative that selects bright graduates of elite colleges and universities for a quick, microwave-oven preparation to teach the nation's children. Looking once again for the pony, one hopes that the comment, politically correct in the setting, was at least faintly tinged with irony. We need the microwave approach to cooking up new teachers quickly to the same degree we need it to supply our new physicians, engineers, and attorneys. We must add to the policy agenda the support of a liberal and professional education for our teachers that prepares them to be moral stewards of robust schools in educative communities.

Clearly, the agenda for the twenty-first century must be more than a policy one; it must be a public one. Given its daunting substance and dimensions, the world context in which it must be advanced makes its implications staggering. We live in the most powerful and most consuming nation on earth and yet have too much social suffering and too much angst. To keep the whole constantly in view while seeking to move forward is to risk the danger that those well prepared to lead will stumble into a pit of angst. It is necessary, however, to keep aware of the whole while planting feet firmly on a chosen path.

Those who participated in our conversation are much-schooled. Their awareness, empathy, and spirit suggest that the schools did not fail them: They are well educated. They contributed to the content and urgency of an educational agenda. There are many others like them who might have been there and who would have embellished the agenda and perhaps added to it. Surely the much-schooled and the well-educated have a special responsibility for advancing an educational agenda that will promote the common good only if it becomes a public one. Many already are assuming this responsibility, but their numbers are relatively small and their voices insufficient.

Most of those who were in the audience of the symposium that constitutes a major part of the foregoing text already have chosen paths that fit comfortably with their life's work and societal need. They represented the Coalition of Essential Schools,[14] committed to the difficult task of creating secondary schools that educate well, and the National Network for Educational Renewal,[15] committed to the simultaneous renewal of schooling and the education of educators. They found common ground in the concept of educating the self in a context of civility and civic communities. Schools must ensure such cultural contexts; teachers must be educated to be their moral stewards. This is the vision—in contrast to that of schools and teachers as providers of a trained workforce—most likely to attract into the teaching profession persons capable of providing the leadership required for the necessary public agenda of education and schooling.

It is a four-part agenda, with each part infused with moral principle. First, our young people must be introduced to and increasingly immersed in the ways of knowing derived from centuries of inquiry into humankind's knowledge systems. That is, they must be introduced to the human conversation that accompanies self-transcendence and, ultimately, identification with humankind. The process of educating involved is personal and more private than public. Second, our young people must be enculturated into the social and political expectations and opportunities of civility and civitas. This process of educating is more public than private. These two components of the agenda constitute the mission of a formal system of education, of which public schooling is a critically important part.

The third and fourth parts pertain to the education of those educators assigned the stewardship of a formal system of education designed to advance the mission defined here. Educators must be thoroughly prepared in the knowledge and propensities required to fulfill this mission of formal education (for example, schooling) in a democratic society. This part of their education is acquired in the liberal studies programs of first-rate colleges and universities. Educators must be thoroughly prepared, also, in the pedagogy required to introduce the young to the human conversation and enculturate them in the moral and civil arts. That is, they must be educated to become moral stewards of the nation's schools.

This four-part agenda is increasingly gaining recognition in renewal-oriented schools aligned with colleges and universities advancing renewal-oriented teacher education programs in initiatives such as that of the National Network for Educational Renewal. The need now is for it to become a public agenda for the renewal of education in the American democracy.

Notes

1. Michael Oakeshott, *Rationalism in Politics and Other Essays* (Indianapolis, Ind.: Liberty Press, 1991), p. 490.
2. See, for example, Mary Catherine Bateson, "Democracy, Ecology, and Participation," in *Democracy, Education, and the Schools*, ed. Roger Soder (San Francisco: Jossey-Bass, 1996), pp. 69–86.

3. Daniel Quinn, *Ishmael* (New York: Bantam, 1992).
4. Jane Roland Martin, "There's Too Much to Teach: Cultural Wealth in an Age of Scarcity," *Educational Researcher* 12 (March 1996): 6.
5. Alexis de Tocqueville, *Democracy in America*, trans. George Lawrence (1835, 1840; reprint, New York: Anchor, 1969), p. 536.
6. Tocqueville, *Democracy in America*, p. 534.
7. Tocqueville, *Democracy in America*, p. 534.
8. Seymour B. Sarason, "American Psychology, and the Needs for Transcendence and Community," *American Journal of Community Psychology* 21 (April 1993): 193.
9. Stephen B. Graubard, "Preface to the Issue 'Social Suffering,'" *Daedalus* 125 (Winter 1996): v.
10. Graubard, "Preface," p. vii.
11. Arthur Kleinman and Joan Kleinman, "The Appeal of Experience; The Dismay of Images: Cultural Appropriations of Suffering in Our Times," *Daedalus* 125 (Winter 1996): 18–19.
12. Kleinman and Kleinman, "The Appeal of Experience," p. 18.
13. David C. Berliner and Bruce J. Biddle, *The Manufactured Crisis: Myths, Fraud, and the Attack on America's Public Schools* (Reading, Mass.: Addison-Wesley, 1995).
14. For information regarding the nature and progress of this initiative, see Theodore R. Sizer, *Horace's School* (Boston: Houghton Mifflin, 1992); and *Horace's Hope* (Boston: Houghton Mifflin, 1996).
15. For information regarding the nature and progress of this initiative, see John I. Goodlad, *Educational Renewal: Better Teachers, Better Schools* (San Francisco: Jossey-Bass, 1994). For its conceptual grounding, see John I. Goodlad, *In Praise of Education* (New York: Teachers College Press, 1997).

3. Daniel Quinn, *Ishmael* (New York: Bantam, 1992).
4. Jane Roland Martin, "There's Too Much to Teach: Cultural Wealth in an Age of Scarcity," *Educational Researcher* 12 (March 1996): 6.
5. Alexis de Tocqueville, *Democracy in America*, trans. George Lawrence (1835, 1840; reprint, New York: Anchor, 1969), p. 536.
6. Tocqueville, *Democracy in America*, p. 534.
7. Tocqueville, *Democracy in America*, p. 534.
8. Seymour B. Sarason, "American Psychology, and the Needs for Transcendence and Community," *American Journal of Community Psychology* 21 (April 1993): 19.
9. Stephen R. Graubard, "Preface to the Issue 'Social Suffering,'" *Daedalus* 125 (Winter 1996): v.
10. Graubard, "Preface," p. vii.
11. Arthur Kleinman and Joan Kleinman, "The Appeal of Experience; The Dismay of Images: Cultural Appropriations of Suffering in Our Times," *Daedalus* 125 (Winter 1996): 18–19.
12. Kleinman and Kleinman, "The Appeal of Experience," p. 18.
13. David C. Berliner and Bruce J. Biddle, *The Manufactured Crisis: Myths, Fraud, and the Attack on America's Public Schools* (Reading, Mass.: Addison-Wesley, 1995).
14. For information regarding the nature and progress of this initiative, see Theodore R. Sizer, *Horace's School* (Boston: Houghton Mifflin, 1992), and *Horace's Hope* (Boston: Houghton Mifflin, 1996).
15. For information regarding the nature and progress of this initiative, see John I. Goodlad, *Educational Renewal: Better Teachers, Better Schools* (San Francisco: Jossey-Bass, 1994). For its conceptual grounding, see John I. Goodlad, *In Praise of Education* (New York: Teachers College Press, 1997).

Additional Readings

Contributors

Contributors to this volume have written widely on educational and social issues. Readers interested in pursuing the themes developed in this collection are encouraged to consult the following publications.

Barber, Benjamin R. *An Aristocracy of Everyone: The Politics of Education and the Future of America*. New York: Ballantine Books, 1992.

An "aristocracy of everyone" is not an oxymoron but precisely what democracy and democratic education are all about. True democracy requires universal education so that all citizens can contribute to and benefit from the social and political system. Education is, in short, the "enabler of democracy" (p. 14).

Darling-Hammond, Linda. "Reframing the School Reform Agenda: Developing Capacity for School Transformation." *Phi Delta Kappan* 74 (June 1993): 752–61.

Our increasingly complex society demands flexibility, problem-solving skills, and resourcefulness. School restructuring efforts must therefore ensure that all students have opportunities to construct knowledge and to develop their talents. New forms of professional development, policy development, and political development can help to create "communities of learning grounded in communities of democratic discourse" (p. 761).

Fenstermacher, Gary D "The Absence of Democratic and Educational Ideals from Contemporary Educational Reform Initiatives." The Stanley Elam Lecture presented to the Educational Press Association of America, 10 June 1994, Chicago, Illinois. Reproduced under the same title in *Educational Horizons* 73 (Winter 1995): 70–80. Also available through ERIC, no. EJ 500 821.

Recent educational reform rhetoric has emphasized economic competition and high standards for schooling but has ignored civic participation and democratic ideals. The rhetoric has the potential to divide the nation rather than to unite it, because improvements will most likely benefit children at the top of the social, economic, and educational scale, while remaining no more than a cruel hoax for lower-status children. Genuine democratic education builds social capital and allows every person to flourish.

Goodlad, John I. *In Praise of Education*. New York: Teachers College Press, 1997.

Education is a personal journey of self-development and self-transcendence, but one that occurs in a specific culture and in a larger environment. The democratic cultural setting of the United States means that education is an inalienable right and that the democratic character must be deliberately cultivated. Not only schools but the entire community must be educative.

Kerr, Donna H. "Democracy, Nurturance, and Community." In Roger Soder, ed., *Democracy, Education, and the Schools*. San Francisco: Jossey-Bass, 1996.

Using schools for instrumental purposes—training young people merely to perform economic or political functions—makes schools dominating, not nurturing, institutions. Nurture is the true moral purpose of schools and must, like civic society, be based on trust and respect for the individual.

McMannon, Timothy J. *Morality, Efficiency, and Reform: An Interpretation of the History of American Education*. Work in Progress Series, no. 5, Institute for Educational Inquiry, 1995.

Educational reform in the United States has typically neglected the moral implications of schooling and concentrated instead on personal, societal, and structural efficiency.

Sizer, Theodore R. *Horace's Hope: What Works for the American High School*. Boston: Houghton Mifflin, 1996.

School reform is difficult but possible. Parents, students, and educators are creating new designs for secondary schooling, often employing the principles of the Coalition of Essential Schools. Students should gain and exhibit deep understanding of a limited number of areas of knowledge rather than be exposed to shallow coverage of a large number of subjects.

Soder, Roger. "Teaching the Teachers of the People." In Roger Soder, ed., *Democracy, Education, and the Schools*. San Francisco: Jossey-Bass, 1996.

Democracy requires that the people—the rulers—be educated and that teachers guide children in the ways of democracy. But only rarely do theorists discuss what, exactly, teachers must know to fulfill this obligation. There are, however, fundamental ideas and essential texts with which teachers should grapple. A suggested list is provided.

Other Authors

Other authors have analyzed themes considered in this book: education, schooling, democracy, society, community. In addition to the writings cited in notes, the following works may be of interest.

Bellah, Robert N., and others. *Habits of the Heart: Individualism and Commitment in American Life*. Berkeley: University of California Press, 1985.

Bellah, Robert N., and others. *The Good Society*. New York: Knopf, 1991.

Gould, Carol C. *Rethinking Democracy: Freedom and Social Cooperation in Politics, Economy, and Society*. Cambridge: Cambridge University Press, 1988.

Jackson, Philip W., Robert E. Boostrom, and David T. Hansen. *The Moral Life of Schools*. San Francisco: Jossey-Bass, 1993.

Kozol, Jonathan. *Savage Inequalities: Children in America's Schools*. New York: Crown, 1991.

Pangle, Thomas L. *The Ennobling of Democracy: The Challenge of the Postmodern Age*. Baltimore: Johns Hopkins University Press, 1992.

Steiner, David M. *Rethinking Democratic Education: The Politics of Reform*. Baltimore: Johns Hopkins University Press, 1994.

Index